New York State's
Mountain Heritage

To Bruce & Susi:

Adirondack Attic
Volume 1

Glad to have met you.
Enjoy exploring the
Adirondack Attic!

June 2004

Andy Flynn's column, "Adirondack Attic,"
can be read every week in the following newspapers:

Adirondack Daily Enterprise, Saranac Lake
Lake Placid News
Press-Republican, Plattsburgh
Post-Star, Glens Falls
News-Enterprise, North Creek (summer only)

New York State's Mountain Heritage

Adirondack Attic
Volume 1

By Andy Flynn

Hungry Bear Publishing
Saranac Lake, New York

New York State's Mountain Heritage:
Adirondack Attic, Volume 1

Copyright © 2004 by Andy Flynn

First Printing

Hungry Bear Publishing
Saranac Lake, New York

Cover design by Andy Flynn
Front cover photo by Richard Walker
Back cover photo of Andy Flynn by Dawn Flynn
Back cover photos of the Adirondack Museum
and the Sunset Cottage rustic panel by Andy Flynn
Artifact photos courtesy of the Adirondack Museum,
Blue Mountain Lake

Distributed by North Country Books
Utica, New York

Library of Congress Control Number: 2004100993

ISBN 0-9754007-0-3

Printed in the United States of America on recycled paper
(85% recovered fiber/30% post consumer)

Book design by Andy Flynn

For Dawn

Contents

photo by Andy Flynn

Relax by the pond in a Westport chair.

Foreword

Within the walls of the Adirondack Museum are century-old tools which harvested trees and earth-bound minerals and ores; vehicles which transported people and goods on land and water; objects from camps and homes; and artifacts which picture the past—thousands of documents from the region, historic photographs, and works of art including paintings, prints and drawings.

Objects document how people lived—elitist and non-elitist. They document the use of materials, the shaping of those materials, and the skill of craftsmen. They document national and regional cultures and the subdivisions within those cultures. Certain classes of objects are readily discernible as New England or Middle Atlantic states or Southwest or, to be more specific, Adirondack, Appalachian, Amish, Shaker, and so on. Artifacts document trade routes, political philosophies, changes in technology and general conditions of life. An object is indicative of the conditions of not only the people who made and used it but also the people for whom it was made.

Objects document attitudes, values and ideas. They document intangibles such as democratic government or law, like local ones in the Adirondacks, and such obviously material ones as manufacturing techniques or transportation. Objects also provide a clue to such subjects as social stratification, family life and the changing role of women in society. The artifact is not always dependent upon the written word for its understanding, shape or conformation. Generally in America, the printed word shaped not only events but also the way things looked. Historians working in museums or historical societies must treat co-equally, as far as possible, the word and the artifact.

The Adirondack Museum collects artifacts, works of art, complete structures, documents, audio and film/video tapes, photographs and printed materials which were made and/or used in the region or which depict the region's people and places. This museum plays a unique role in the cultural and intellectual life of the Adirondacks as the major repository for material and archival documents of the region's social and cultural history. This material residue documents the people who lived here and the ways that they made their livings.

Andy Flynn began his odyssey behind the scenes in the collections at the Adirondack Museum in 2003. His goal was to make connections between people and their pasts through the historic artifacts collected by the Museum. His newspaper articles gathered in this volume provide a window on the history that enriches the experience of the objects for visitors when they visit the Museum or its storage collections.

Andy has very generously donated part of the proceeds from this book to support the Museum's Collection Improvement Fund, a restricted fund for contributions to support the purchase and care of collections. The Adirondack Museum is grateful to Andy Flynn for supporting the work of the Museum to collect, preserve and interpret the past.

Caroline M. Welsh
Chief Curator
The Adirondack Museum

Preface

When I first pitched the idea of an "Adirondack Attic" column to Adirondack Museum officials in the fall of 2002, it was just a pipe dream. Write a weekly column, self-syndicate it by selling it to newspapers throughout the state, save money and write a book. That was the plan, and I've had to pinch myself every week since the Museum said "yes" to the idea. This book is evidence that dreams do come true.

Five newspapers in the Adirondack region answered the call to run the "Adirondack Attic" during its first year, with a weekly circulation of almost 70,000. Loyal readers turn to the column every Thursday, Friday or Sunday to see what I will dig up next.

The duty of choosing the artifacts rests on the shoulders of the Adirondack Museum staff and myself. I work with the curatorial department to find fascinating objects, some with extensive history attached and some with just a dribble of background. My mission is to turn a picture and a few notes into a story about New York state's mountain heritage and our unique way of life in the 6-million-acre Adirondack Park.

Seasons are extremely important in the Adirondack Mountains. In addition to winter, spring, summer and fall, we have to endure mud season in March and April and bug season in May and June. Some people say summer is only as long as one day—the Fourth of July. Others don't celebrate fall; they call it hunting season, which lasts from September to December (longer for those who hunt small game). The extreme weather in the Adirondacks is a constant butt of jokes, but that's the way we deal with it. In the winter we say, "At least there aren't any bugs." In the summer we say, "At least it's not snowing." (That's on the off-chance it really isn't snowing.)

The tourism-based economy and special events in the Adirondacks are determined by the weather. Therefore, the "Adirondack Attic" is designed to reflect the seasonal flow. Snowshoe forms and woodstoves in the winter, hiking and camping equipment in the summer and hunting gear in the fall. We celebrated Teddy Roosevelt Weekend in the town of Newcomb in September with an artifact from TR's famous "Night Ride to the Presidency" in 1901. We highlighted artifacts in new exhibits when the Museum opened for the season in May.

Since the Adirondack Museum owns more than 100,000 artifacts, most are currently in storage. The "Adirondack Attic" features objects that are in storage and on display. The focus, however, is on the artifacts that are tucked away, hence the "Attic" metaphor.

The name of the column conjures up images of old stuff piled high in an attic collecting dust, but nothing could be farther from the truth. The Adirondack Museum is a state-of-the-art facility that employs well-trained staff to collect, organize and properly store artifacts so they can interpret the history of the Adirondack Mountains. There's a reason the New York Times calls it "the best of its kind in the world."

I am grateful the Museum staff lets me in the door every month to poke around and find stories to tell the public. I am no historian; my background is in journalism, so I rely on research and interviews to tell these stories in newspaper format trying my best to stick with The Associated Press style.

The column's goal is to tell human stories behind artifacts at the Adirondack Museum, and each story is different. The amount of history available in the accession file determines the storytelling direction. If there is a lot of information about the people who used the artifact (Edward Earl and the beam knife), I lean toward the human history. If there is little information in the file, I may explore an industry (spruce gum harvesting) or a movement (Arts and Crafts Movement) that helps answer the question, "Who are these Adirondack people?"

In some columns, artifacts have provenances outside the Blue Line ("Grand Gold Coin" range stove). That doesn't mean they are unimportant to Adirondack history. The Adirondack Museum collection includes and represents objects that were once used in the Park. In some cases, I dare to venture outside the bubble we live in and tell stories about other places. This is a conscious effort to show that we all came from somewhere else at one point in our lineage. In the grand scheme of history, even the natives are outsiders.

In all cases, the "Adirondack Attic" attempts to present a unique way of life found nowhere else in New York, the United States or even the world. People come from all corners of the globe, such as China and Italy, to study the great experiment we call the Adirondack Park.

The Adirondack Mountain range is the biggest in the state, and the Adirondack Park is the largest state park in the lower 48. A patchwork of public and private lands representing parts of 12 counties, it is roughly the size of Vermont.

The "Adirondack Attic" tells the story of New York state's mountain heritage, one chapter at a time.

Andy Flynn

Acknowledgments

Germinating the "Adirondack Attic" seed at the Adirondack Museum was Ann Carroll, the former director of publicity who left in June 2003. We spoke about the idea at the Adirondack Tourism Conference in Lake Placid in November 2002, and by the new year, I had written a pilot column to send to newspaper editors and publishers. Thanks to her support, we were able to create a unique partnership that ultimately fulfills our mutual goal: teaching the public about New York state's Adirondack Mountain heritage on a weekly basis. The partnership allows the column to sustain itself while offering the Museum well-deserved publicity. I have known Ann professionally for more than a decade, and I long for her broad smile and keen sense of humor.

It was also tough to see Adirondack Museum Curator Jane Mackintosh leave in the summer of 2003. Jane drafted the first list of "Attic" artifacts to be studied, and she provided much-needed expertise for the pilot column—the multiple-iron laundry stove featured in Chapter 2. There is no doubt that my early articles were improved by her attention to detail. Jane's vast knowledge of everything Adirondack is sorely missed, and I wish her the best in her new chapter of life.

Adirondack Museum Director John Collins, who left the facility in February 2004, was continually supportive of the "Adirondack Attic" column and the 2003 compilation. It was sad when he departed, but I'm sure I'll see him around. He has the energy of a teenager and a passionate love for the Adirondacks that will likely keep him active in the fight to preserve the mountains his family has called home for generations.

When the front doors of the Adirondack Museum close for the season in October, a great many people think the campus goes dormant and the workers hibernate for the winter. Lies, all lies. The back doors of the Museum remain open, and the staff continues to upgrade the facilities, offer educational activities to school children, dismantle outgoing exhibits, maintain current exhibits, plan for upcoming exhibits, acquire new artifacts, maintain the collection, help researchers, raise funds to keep the Museum open, etc. The work is non-stop and exhausting, and the dedication of Museum employees to keep the Adirondack Mountain heritage alive is unwavering. I tip my hat to each and every one of them.

My name may be attached to the "Adirondack Attic" column, but it takes a dedicated team to pull it off every week. Monthly visits to Blue Mountain Lake are filled with finding the right artifacts, collecting the accession files and other written material for research, taking photographs of the objects or tracking down pre-existing jpegs to send to the newspapers, and planning for future trips to the Museum. My time is spent with Collections Manager Tracy Meehan, Librarian Jerry Pepper, Chief Curator and Director of Operations Caroline Welsh, Curator Hallie Bond, Angela Donnelly and Doreen Alessi. I am continually inspired by their professionalism.

Extra gratitude is extended to Caroline Welsh for writing the foreword to "Volume 1" and for always being supportive of my writing efforts with the Adirondack Museum. She is a first-class lady and a great asset to the Museum and the entire Adirondack Park. Caroline is mentioned several times in this book, sometimes because of the regional books she has either edited or written.

The editor-writer relationship is typified by the ideological friction caused by the duties of each: an editor focusing on the bigger picture while keeping the writer away from the English language pitfalls in grammar, punctuation, usage, capitalization, style, etc.; and a writer fighting hard to maintain creative expression while mustering enough courage to say "you're right" once in a while. Pride needs to be swallowed on both ends, as it can never take a backseat to honesty in this business. Hopefully tact can prevail and the writer and editor will find themselves talking again sometime soon.

In a perfect world, editor corrects writer, writer agrees and makes revisions.

The mother-son relationship is typified by the ideological friction caused by the duties of each: a mother focusing on the bigger picture while keeping the son away from making an idiot of himself; and a son fighting hard to maintain creative expression while mustering enough courage to say "you're right" once in a while.

When it came time to edit "Volume 1," I needed someone I could trust to catch my mistakes and be blunt enough to tell me about them. Luckily, my mother, a former teacher, has a lot of experience correcting my mistakes, and she didn't find it difficult to be blunt. To our amazement, we were able to discuss the text like publishing professionals, and we both made concessions. She didn't make me cry once, probably because I agreed with most of her suggestions. And I appreciate that. (She hates when I start a sentence with "And.")

In all seriousness, it was a pleasure to work with my mom, Michele Flynn, and I hope we can collaborate on more projects in the future. Just a tip, if you want to get along with her, always call me

"Andrew." She doesn't have a son named "Andy."

My beautiful wife, Dawn (who does call me Andy), is a goddess. Who else could put up with my zany ideas and projects? She walks around with a knot in her stomach that reads, "What the hell will he come up with next? Lord, help me." This book is dedicated to Dawn for almost eight years of support and tolerance, through journalism and public relations careers and now during a quest to be a self-published writer.

Thanks to my twin brother, Steve, who I wish had been my best friend growing up instead of my competitor. We're either too much alike or too different to make that happen now. Ironically, the distance between Colorado and New York has brought us closer than ever, probably because we're out of swinging distance from each other. I cannot match his artistic talents and I thank him for creating the logo for Hungry Bear Publishing. He paints pet potraits and murals, too, for those who want to tap into his mountain-inspired creativity.

To the editors and publishers who took a chance on me in 2003, thank you for everything. None of this would be possible without the syndication of the "Adirondack Attic" column in newspapers around the Adirondack North Country region.

Lastly, thanks to the readers who visit me each week on printed pages for a visit to the Adirondack Museum in Blue Mountain Lake. It has been extremely gratifying to speak to readers who have related to the artifacts due to their own heirlooms and family connections to the objects. There is nothing more satisfying to a columnist to hear, "I read your column faithfully each week." Over the past year, I have heard that phrase many times, and those words fuel my curiosity engine and inspire me to keep exploring the "Adirondack Attic."

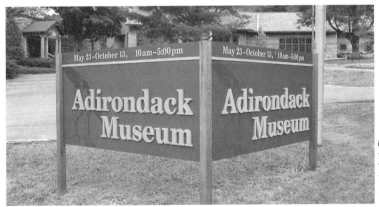

Adirondack Museum sign on Route 30 as seen in 2003

Chapter 1

Explore history in the Adirondack Attic

Adirondack Museum Collections Manager Tracy Meehan handed me a plastic bag full of sterile, white gloves, the kind they use to handle delicate artifacts. I plucked out two and stretched the extra-small gloves on my extra-large hands. It was a defining moment; I was ready to explore the Adirondack Attic.

A few months ago, I enjoyed watching a Joan Lunden program on the A&E cable channel. It was a behind-the-scenes look at the Smithsonian Institution museums in Washington, D.C., affectionately called "America's Attic." Curators led her through the many temperature- and humidity-controlled corridors that are off-limits to the general public. She took a sneak peek at thousands of artifacts that are basically in storage for posterity, some waiting to be placed in exhibits and others that will never be on display.

That gave me an idea. Why not rummage through the Adirondack Attic—the Adirondack Museum in Blue Mountain Lake—and tell stories about those artifacts in storage and in the exhibits?

After all, heritage tourism continues to grow in the Adirondack region, a trend noted by the Adirondack Regional Tourism Council's recent publication called Adirondack Yesteryears. The booklet is a guide to Adirondack historical sites, museums and events in New York state's Adirondack North Country region.

Whether people are obsessively curious or just plain nosy, their fascination with historical materials is evident with the popularity of places like the Smithsonian Institution museums, television programs such as the "Antiques Roadshow" and sophisticated features on the History Channel and A&E.

The "Adirondack Attic" will feature an artifact each week from the Adirondack Museum, and I will connect the objects to the people who settled the Adirondack Mountains. By making that human connection with the artifacts, we'll be able to give these objects life and tell the story of the Adirondack Park one tiny chapter at a time. This is a chance for readers to discover New York's mountain heritage and explore their own history.

The "Adirondack Attic" will not be an antiques column, and we will not talk about the price value of items. They are historical artifacts, not antiques.

Called "the best of its kind in the world" by the New York Times,

Adirondack Museum Curator Jane Mackintosh looks for a pair of George Capron's snowshoes.

(Photo by Andy Flynn)

the internationally renowned Adirondack Museum overlooks Blue Mountain Lake. Almost 6 million acres of Adirondack Park surround the facility and form the basis of the Museum's exhibits and programs, telling the stories of how people have lived, worked, played and traveled in the Adirondack region since the early 1800s.

While curators are instrumental in finding suitable artifacts for this column every week, readers should know that I do not work for the Adirondack Museum. This is a freelance project. I have written for various newspapers in the North Country for almost 10 years, including the Plattsburgh Press-Republican, and I am a former staff writer and editor of the Lake Placid News and Adirondack Daily Enterprise.

Next week, we'll explore our first artifact, a multiple-iron laundry stove that serviced the Ausable Club in the early 20th century before it was used by the late Keene Valley painter Harold Weston in his home studio. Weston and his wife donated the stove to the Adirondack Museum in 1956. It has since been on display two separate times, once in the 1950s and another time in 1998 for the "Keeping Warm & Keeping Cold" exhibit where the Museum celebrated the rural traditions of wood burning and ice harvesting.

Chapter 2

Multiple-iron laundry stove

Modernist landscape painter Harold Weston was barely a year old when the JL Mott Iron Works hot cast its first 1895 laundry stove in Troy. Twenty-five years later, that stove kept him warm during his maiden Adirondack winter near Keene Valley. It was the end of the laundry stove's career and the beginning of Weston's. They wouldn't part for another 36 years.

In 1956, Weston and his wife donated a multiple-iron laundry stove to the Adirondack Museum and was tagged artifact No. 56.76.1.

"It was clearly used in a hotel that had a busy season for laundry, sheets, and table linens," said Adirondack Museum Curator Jane Mackintosh, noting the size of the appliance.

Prior to 1920, the stove was part of the linen-pressing operation at the Ausable Club. It holds about 20 irons, which rest at an angle and are heated by the burning wood inside.

The laundry stove is stored at the Adirondack Museum with thousands of other artifacts from rural life in northern New York state. It is on a wheeled, wooden cart in the Homesteading Section of the archives, flanked on the right by a Curtis moldboard plow and on the left by a smaller laundry stove once owned by William West Durant at Camp Pine Knot on Raquette Lake. Behind is a large, iron cauldron.

The JL Mott Iron Works used iron, possibly from the Adirondacks, to make its line of 19th century appliances, which were state-of-the-art in those days. The stove's model name, "No. 1 Improved 1895," can be read on the front bottom lip, below the air-control vents.

A couple of miles east of Keene Valley in Essex County is the hamlet of St. Huberts, the home of the Ausable Club and a popular trailhead for hikers entering the High Peaks, Giant Mountain and Dix Mountain wilderness areas.

That's where the Beede family opened a hostelry for summer tourists in the late 1800s. The hotel was razed by fire in March 1890, but the Beedes quickly built the St. Hubert's Inn on the same site, opening for the season on July 15. The three-story Victorian inn, named for the patron saint of hunted deer, still stands today. In 1906, the hotel was sold to the Adirondack Mountain Reserve and renamed the Ausable Club.

It's not clear when or how the laundry stove was purchased, but it had to be after 1895. The JL Mott Iron Works published illustrated

Multiple-iron laundry stove, artifact No. 56.76.1, circa 1895

(Photo courtesy of the Adirondack Museum)

catalogs and sold many household items, including stoves, ornamental fountains, bath tubs and other plumbing supplies. Similar to today's business practices (minus the realm of e-commerce), the Beedes may have ordered the stove from a catalog and had it delivered to the hotel.

The stove's parts were most likely shipped in wooden crates by train to Port Henry and transported by a horse-drawn wagon to the St. Hubert's Inn, where it was probably assembled. According to Eleanor Alderson Janeway's recollection in 1951, Fletcher Beede had picked up her family at the D&H railroad station in Port Henry in August 1887 and driven them 35 miles to Beede's House in "a high brake with four horses" along the narrow Chapel Pond dirt road (now Route 73).

The stove and other supplies probably made the same journey.

"When the laundry building was being torn down to clear space for the Ausable Club pool in 1920, the stove was given to me when living as a bachelor here for three years," Weston wrote in a 1956 letter to the Adirondack Museum.

In 1920, Weston wintered alone at his Ausable Club studio to start his painting career. In his autobiography, "Freedom in the Wilds," Weston recalls that first winter: "The walls of my studio were made of rough native hemlock, the framework of spruce. There was no insulation ... The pot-bellied box stove I kept stoked with two-foot lengths so the fire in it only went out once or twice during the winter months."

The laundry stove has been on display at the Adirondack Museum two separate times. The last time was in 1998 during the "Keeping Warm & Keeping Cold" exhibit, where the Museum celebrated the rural traditions of wood burning and ice harvesting.

As a security measure, the irons were welded on to the stove before it was first exhibited in the 1950s. That type of practice is frowned upon today, according to Mackintosh, who said the Museum would not do anything to an artifact that cannot be reversed (e.g. stripping original paint from a wooden dresser). If the Museum were to receive the stove today, curators might simply place irons on it and rope an area around the artifacts so people don't touch them.

The antique irons attached to the stove came from several places in the Adirondack region: Raquette Lake, Wevertown, Newcomb, Poland and St. Huberts.

"If you had 16 irons on the stove, one would always be hot," Mackintosh explained. "Not that you would have that many people ironing, but it allowed several people to work quickly at the same time."

Chapter 3

Snowshoe-making forms

The story of George Capron is typical of the Adirondack region. Like many mountain men in the 19th and 20th centuries (and even today), he had at least two seasonal jobs to make ends meet.

Capron was a stone mason by trade. In Big Moose, his summer job included brick laying and cement work, and while some of the buildings he helped construct may still be standing in the Big Moose area, it's his winter job that we remember the most.

Capron made snowshoes. His workshop in the Oneida County village of Boonville was filled with wooden forms, bow stock and bent ash and was equipped with a wood stove to keep him warm through the frigid, snowy winters between the Adirondack Mountains and the Tug Hill Plateau. He worked alone.

Boonville, a gateway to the Adirondacks and only 30 miles southwest of Old Forge, is in the Black River Valley, a fitting location for making wooden snowshoes since it was one of the chief lumber towns in the North Country. Boonville is still home to the New York State Woodsmen's Field Days every third weekend in August.

Back in Capron's day, snowshoes were made more for necessity than recreation. Hunters, trappers, lumberjacks, mail carriers and others required the use of snowshoes for their jobs. Today, the story is much different. Snowshoeing is North America's fastest growing winter recreational sport. The makers of aluminum and plastic Tubbs, Atlas and MSR snowshoes have probably never heard of early 20th century craftsmen such as George Capron. In his day, though, he was the king of snowshoe making in Boonville.

Many of Capron's snowshoes were sent to Maine for sale, yet the pair he made for a Boonville man was the vital link between his craftsmanship and the Adirondack Museum.

The woman who donated a number of Capron's snowshoe forms and other materials from his workshop in 1990 had owned a pair of Brinckerhoff Model snowshoes (oval-shaped bearpaw) made for her father.

The snowshoe form we're examining today, artifact No. 90.22.18, is an extra small type A form for a Capron model snowshoe (currently in storage). On the form itself are the words "Extra Small Cap" written in pencil script.

Capron made snowshoes on a regular basis from 1909 until his

George Capron snowshoe form, artifact No. 90.22.18

(Photo courtesy of the Adirondack Museum)

death in 1934. He was also a salesman, having 10 of his models featured in a one-page catalog. The front of the flyer read "George O. Capron, Maker of High Grade Snow Shoes."

The models, in specific order, were as follows: 1. Woods Model; 2. Frost Model; 3. Church Model; 4. Brinckerhoff Model; 5. Brown Model; 6. Crego Model; 7. Boyer Model—Gents; 8. Boyer Model—Ladies; 9. Capron Model; and 10. Syphert Model.

The Adirondack Museum owns 23 of Capron's wooden forms for a variety of snowshoe styles and sizes, unbent bow stock, bent bows (bent ash for use in snowshoe making), a form for making skipjacks, measuring devices (yard sticks and dowels incrementally marked), a wash boiler (a metal washtub with a hinged lid) and a square metal steam box that fits inside the boiler. Some of the forms have years written on them in pencil, but artifact No. 90.22.18 does not. The Museum also owns several fur-stretching boards once used by Capron's son, Robert.

The headline of Capron's obituary read "Well Known Snowshoe Maker Found Dead in Bed in Early Morning." At the age of 71, his wife found him dead of natural causes when she went to his room to call on him. That was Aug. 13, 1934.

"He was a member of the Baptist Church and was a respected citizen," stated the obituary.

Capron was born on March 20, 1863 in Leyden and apparently made snowshoes for at least 60 years, according to his records. We only highlight his last 25 years of snowshoe making, starting in 1909, perhaps because that's the year he settled down for good.

In his younger days, Capron worked in Buffalo Bill's Wild West Show as a cowboy and a hitch man and in the Washburn Circus. He gave it up when he married Mrs. William Cummings Alger, of Lowville, on Sept. 29, 1909. They had two children.

Chapter 4

Zoetrope

Today we have endless forms of entertainment to keep us busy during this dreary March weather. Adirondackers can rent videos and DVDs, turn on cable television, surf the Internet or trek through the snow and slush to the Hotel Saranac on Wednesday night to see movies in the Saranac Lake Cabin Fever Classic Film Festival.

The days of the Zoetrope are long gone.

Prior to the movies, and even before there was an Adirondack Park, pre-cinema contraptions like the Zoetrope entertained families in the post-Civil War era.

The Adirondack Museum owns a 13-slot Zoetrope (artifact No. 2002.43.1) and several double-sided paper animated strips, including one named the "Star Spangled Banner" (artifact No. 2002.43.5). The strips are 3.5 inches tall and 36 inches long and have a series of pictures painted on them. When a strip is placed in the Zoetrope, and the drum is spun, it produces a moving subject that appears to progress forward—a crude motion picture. In "Star Spangled Banner," a man is pounding a hammer on top of a flagpole. On the reverse side, a top spins in circles in "A Tip Top Thing."

An English mathematician, William Horner, invented the first Zoetrope in 1840, calling it the "daedaleum." Milton Bradley, a Massachusetts lithographer and game inventor, was granted a patent in 1867 and began manufacturing the Zoetrope the same year. The Milton Bradley toy company later made popular games such as Twister and Candy Land and the electronic gizmo Simon.

The side of the cylinder is made of heavy brown paper with long, narrow sides for viewing the animated strips. The bottom is a round piece of wood that is attached to the sides by nails. The cylinder is attached to a wooden base by a metal spindle and shaft. On the bottom of the base is a red paper label that reads "The Zoetrope, or Wheel of Life. Manufactured solely by Milton Bradley & Co., Springfield, Mass. Patented April 1867." The toy also includes directions for operation.

The Zoetrope works by placing one of the animated strips around the inside of the cylinder with its lower edging resting on the bottom. The cylinder, which rotates at an angle, is then spun, and the rotation speed may vary for different pictures. The paper cylinder looks like an upside down lamp shade with vertical 4-inch-tall (1/2 inch wide) slots

Milton Bradley Zoetrope and animated strip, artifacts 2002.43.1 and 2002.43.5, circa 1867

(Photo courtesy of the Adirondack Museum)

cut every 3 inches. The best effects are with a light source lighting the interior of the cylinder. In all, the Zoetrope is 11.5 inches tall.

This motion picture invention was groundbreaking for its day; moving scenes could finally be viewed by multiple people, each standing 3 to 6 feet away and looking through the slots. It pre-dated single-viewing devices such as the magic lantern.

Other animated strips include the "French Revolution," which depicts a person removing his own head from his body and passing it to a man next to him. The reverse side is labeled "Jack in the Box," where a head pops out of a green box. The "Gymnast" strip shows a man jumping backward through a hoop (or forward, depending how you spin the cylinder). On the reverse side, a dog catches a ball in its mouth in "Old Dog Tray."

A descendent of Elizabethtown Judge Augustus N. Hand (1869-1954) donated the Zoetrope in the summer of 2002. The judge used it when he was a child in the 1870s, and the toy was inherited through generations of the Hand family.

Hand was born on July 26, 1869 in the Essex County town of Elizabethtown. He was a judge of the U.S. District Court for the Southern District of New York, 1914-27, and a judge of the U.S. Court of Appeals for the 2nd Circuit, 1927-53. He died on Oct. 28, 1954.

The judge's grandfather was Augustus C. Hand (1803-1878), a prominent politician and judge, serving as a member of the U.S. Congress from 1839 to 1841 and the New York State Senate from 1845 to 1848 and a New York State Supreme Court justice from 1848 to 1855. The grandfather's River Street home, built in 1849, is now part of Elizabethtown's Hand-Hale Historic District. It is a brick Greek Revival structure.

A portrait of Augustus N. Hand hangs in the historic 1885 courtroom at the Essex County Government Center, in the same room where the 18-member Essex County Board of Supervisors meet.

The judge was buried in an Elizabethtown cemetery. The Zoetrope remains in storage at the Adirondack Museum. Milton Bradley is now a division of Hasbro, Inc.

Chapter 5

Crazy quilt

When Mary Church Holland's first child died, she was in emotional agony. On the advice of her doctor, who told her to "keep busy," she made an award-winning crazy quilt. That was 1887-88.

Mamie, as she was known, lived in the Warren County hamlet of North River as a school teacher and an artist, and the men in her family worked at Hooper's Garnet Mines. The crazy quilt won prizes at a number of state fairs, but it was never used as an actual coverlet. Mamie later had three more children: Lynn, Vera and Lyle Holland.

Her heirloom quilt is now artifact No. 92.50 in the Adirondack Museum's collection.

The quilt's dimensions are 71-by-54.5 inches, and it has brown twill cotton backing. The "crazy" patches are silk, velvet, satin and brocade. They are all varying sizes, some decorated with embroidery and paint, and they are sewn to unbleached muslin with a wide variety of stitches. Mamie embroidered the date and her initials into one of the corners.

The fabric in the quilt has become somewhat worn over the years and has never been repaired. It is extremely delicate and remains carefully stored in a box. When it was received in 1992, it was in good condition, but some swatches were deteriorated. It was vacuumed, removing cat hair from the surface.

The crazy quilt was donated by one of Mamie's great-great-granddaughters from New Jersey who had received it from her great-aunt, Vivian Monthony Morris, one of Mamie's granddaughters.

Morris was born in North River in 1925 and moved to New Jersey the same year. Writing to her great-niece from Florida in her retirement years, Morris outlined her last wishes, including the passing of this heirloom.

"(Mamie) was your great-great-grandmother. She died in the great flu epidemic in the first world war," Morris wrote. "As you are the direct descendant on my side of the family, I thought you might like to have it."

Morris asked that the quilt either be handed down to other generations or donated to the "Blue Mountain Museum, Blue Mountain Lake, New York State in the Adirondacks."

In her correspondence to the curator, the donor said the staff and facilities of the Adirondack Museum could take better care of the quilt.

North River crazy quilt, artifact No. 92.50, circa 1888

(Photo courtesy of the Adirondack Museum)

"I'm afraid it is not being cared for properly," she said, adding that it was important that this artifact be preserved.

The crazy quilt style features randomly cut and sewn scraps of silk, velvet, brocade, plush satin, wool, cotton and linen. It was a wildly popular Victorian pastime that had it roots at the Centennial Exposition of 1876 in Philadelphia. One of the exhibits at the Exposition's Japanese pavilion included crazed ceramics and asymmetrical art. This Japanese style had a profound impact on American culture and influenced the hobby of quilt making, which more middle and upper class women were trying during the Industrial Revolution. Increased wealth gave these women the means to hire help to perform mundane household chores, thus giving them more free time.

Crazy quilts were made for decoration rather than function. Some were made as lap robes and others were hung as show pieces in the parlor. Many, such as the one Mamie Church Holland created, were passed on from generation to generation. Some families added their own patches—even scraps of wedding dress material—to their quilts.

Quilting is a popular contemporary hobby in the Adirondacks, and many women and children in villages such as Newcomb and Tupper Lake have formed clubs to showcase their work. Members of the

Raquette River Quilters, for example, give shows at the Goff-Nelson Memorial Library in Tupper Lake, and members of the Newcomb Mountain Quilters continue this rural tradition by holding workshops and demonstrations at the New York State Adirondack Park Agency Visitor Interpretive Center in Newcomb.

One member of the Newcomb Mountain Quilters, Linda Bennett, gives quilting demonstrations each summer at the Adirondack Museum. A substitute teacher at the Newcomb Central School, she lives in North River, and her husband works at the historic Barton (garnet) Mines.

Chapter 6

Ivory aide memoire

Today VIPs can check their leather-bound Filofax day planners or electronic Palm Pilots to find out where they need to be for lunches and meetings. On the road, that appointment book is even more important, especially for prominent businessmen and politicians who need to be organized to retain their wealth and power.

It was essential even in the early 1800s, when professionals had never heard of PDAs, PCs or lithium-polymer rechargeable batteries. Archibald McIntyre was this kind of man. Hailing from Albany, he was a member of New York state's Assembly and Senate and was the state's comptroller from 1805 to 1821. McIntyre was also a wealthy businessman and invested his money in projects all over the United States. He would surely need to be organized on his business trips to the Adirondack Mountains.

McIntyre, known mostly for his role in establishing the iron works at Tahawus in the Essex County town of Newcomb, owned an aide memoire (also spelled aide d'memoire or l'aide d'memoire). It is a petite day-minder notebook accompanied by a writing utensil that held a lead piece. Made of ivory and metal, they are artifacts No. 2002.45.3 a/b at the Adirondack Museum's collection (currently in storage).

The notebook itself is fascinating. It is 2.75 inches tall and 1.75 inches wide and can easily fit inside a suit pocket. Instead of today's paper sheets, this day-planner had thin ivory wafers for six days of the week, Monday through Saturday. The names of the days are engraved at the top of each page, and the pages fan out to reveal the contents. A rivet at the base holds all the pieces together, including the thicker front and back. Other models of this ivory aide memoire had covers and backs made of mother-of-pearl. Even though it still fans out from the bottom, this particular artifact is missing the latch that held the pages together at the top.

The pencil has an ivory handle with a metal fitting for lead. McIntyre simply wrote his engagements on the ivory pages and wiped them off with water and a cloth after the appointments were over. Records at the Adirondack Museum reveal that McIntyre used this aide memoire at the Tahawus iron mine in the early 19th century.

McIntyre was born in Scotland in 1772 and died in Albany in 1858. In addition to his political career, he had a number of investments: a coal mine in Pennsylvania, the gold rush in North Carolina in

Ivory aide memoire, artifact No. 2002.45.3 a/b

(Photo courtesy of the Adirondack Museum)

the 1840s, cotton mills in Broadalbin and Auburn and property in five Midwest states.

McIntyre's first Adirondack investment was made in 1809 in the Essex County town of North Elba when he and two partners, Malcolm McMartin and David Henderson, bought a water-power utility on the Chubb River, according to Alfred Donaldson's book, "The History of the Adirondacks, Volume 1." Iron ore had been discovered near Lake Placid, and the men built a forge and founded the Elba Iron Works. The place was abandoned in 1815.

In 1826, a Native American man showed the potential investors an iron ore deposit on the other side of Indian Pass, in the town of Newcomb. It was at the site of the current ghost town known as Adirondac or McIntyre. Backcountry enthusiasts heading into the eastern High Peaks from the south know it as the Upper Works. It is a popular trailhead, leading hikers to wilderness destinations such as the Indian Pass, Flowed Lands and Mount Marcy—New York's highest peak at 5,344 feet.

The state's second highest mountain, Algonquin Peak, was originally named after McIntyre, and the range that includes Algonquin, Boundary and Iroquois—all peaks over 4,000 feet—make up what is commonly known as the "MacIntyre" Range. These mountains can also be accessed via the Upper Works trailhead.

By the early 1830s, McIntyre was again the leader of a new iron ore venture, which was often called the McIntyre Iron Works. The operations began near Henderson Lake in 1832, and the Lower Works dwellings, dam and sawmill were built about 10 miles to the south along the Hudson River and the shores of Lake Sanford (where the National Lead Industries started mining titanium dioxide in the early 1940s). This area is called Tahawus.

In 1834, they abandoned their efforts and only regained interest after the New York State Geological Survey commenced in 1837, according to Bruce Seely, who wrote a history on the Adirondack Iron & Steel Company. The survey indicated a high quality of ore, and therefore, work continued at the McIntyre mine in 1838. By 1843, men at the Upper Works were turning out from 12 to 14 tons of iron a day, and more than 100 people were employed there.

Transportation problems and failure in the iron-making process, however, led to the mine's demise by 1856. Ironically, one of the impurities in the ore—titanium dioxide—was needed in the paint-making industry for the military in World War II. The government finally built a railroad to Tahawus and opened the Sanford mine in 1941. Mining operations closed in the 1980s.

Chapter 7

Baseball jerseys

It's early April, and the snowy Adirondack weather is great for snowshoe softball. But who's in the mood for snowshoe softball? Baseball fans yearn for the sweet smell of grass growing in the outfield, the touch of new-found sunshine on our short-sleeved shirts and the hounding sound of an umpire barking, "Play ball!"

High school pitchers are stuck inside their living rooms, perched nervously on hardwood chairs, staring outside their frosty windows while oiling their gloves. They can taste the leather. They get antsy. Varsity baseball sluggers, practicing in indoor cages, adjust batting gloves and scratch their itchy palms. At night, they dream about finding the sweet spot on their aluminum bats. They're all home run kings, and soon they will be chasing hardballs in the mud, snow, wind and rain. The brief high school baseball season is unforgiving, and always messy, in the Adirondacks.

Big-leaguers, on the other hand, have already finished spring training and returned north to their summer home fields (a little Baltimore snow doesn't hurt anyone on opening day). When it's 80 degrees in Florida, we all get a little jealous. Summer must be on its way, or spring at least.

Today, softball is king here in the summer. Adults yearning for the crack of a bat settle for the "chink" of a slow-pitched ball as they pound it out of the park with metal fatties. Our boys of summer are much different than those prior to World War II.

Old-timers pine for the glory days on dusty Adirondack infields. In the first half of the 20th century, North Country towns had their own adult baseball teams and played each other for bragging rights throughout the summer. Newspapers were full of these accounts.

On Aug. 31, 1939, the Adirondack Arrow reported, "The Newcomb baseball team administered a sound beating to the Long Lake boys Sunday. Final score was 4-3."

In 1992, some of those baseball memories were donated to the Adirondack Museum in the form of baseball jerseys (pants, shirts, undergarments and socks) by John and Anita Schmidt, of Jamesville, N.Y. After buying the Raquette Lake camp once owned by the late George Moore, they found the baseball memorabilia in the attic. Moore had played for the Raquette Lake team.

These jerseys, from Adirondack hamlets such as Long Lake, Old

Long Lake baseball jersey, artifact No. 92.35.1

(Photo courtesy of the Adirondack Museum)

Forge and Raquette Lake, date from the late 1930s.

The Long Lake baseball jersey, artifact No. 92.35.1, still has sweat stains around the neck, and the pant legs have dirt across the front. You can just picture an Adirondack slugger sliding into home plate and dusting off his shirt and legs after the umpire yells, "Safe!" (He's safe until he gets home and his wife tries to get the stains out.) It's the well-worn character of these uniforms that give them historical value.

This particular jersey is a heather gray wool, button down, short-sleeved shirt with blue pinstripes. There is extra material in the armpit with six reinforced ventilation holes, and the shirt has blue flannel lettering with "Long Lake" on the front and "Altamont/Milk Co." on the back. The Altamont Milk Company was based in Tupper Lake. The pants had the same material, with one large and three small belt loops around the waist.

The Adirondack Museum has several other baseball artifacts, including a baseball jersey from the Old Forge Fire Department and one from Raquette Lake. The Old Forge shirt is heather gray wool with red flannel lettering, and the Raquette Lake shirt is heather gray wool with maroon flannel lettering.

From the 1890s to the 1940s, the Adirondack region was filled with teams that played "serious weekend baseball," according to a 1992 "Speaking Artifactually" column in the Museum's newsletter.

"Between the wars most towns fielded at least one adult team ... Winning teams practiced nearly every day. Spirited town rivalries created standards of team performance and fan participation that are rarely seen on contemporary softball fields."

In the 1920s, "Prince Hal" Schumacher was a favorite pitcher in Old Forge, retiring young from baseball in the Adirondacks to climb the rungs of Major League Baseball. He pitched 12 seasons for the New York Giants.

"Half of the Giants' famed righty/lefty pitching duo with Hall of Fame'er 'King Carl' Hubbell, Prince Hal won 23 games in 1934," the Museum's article stated.

Chapter 8

A.F. Tait's mould planer

In 1957, a picture-frame planer originally owned by a well-known 19th century painter was donated to the Adirondack Museum. It came by the way of New York City, from a donor who worked in the Kennedy Galleries, and there was a paper label on the side of the woodworking tool.

It was no secret which famous painter had once owned the artifact. Still, when curators removed the label in the year 2000, they were pleasantly surprised by what was underneath.

The planer (artifact No. 57.137) is inscribed with A.F. Tait's signature, believed to be "by himself in the handwriting which he used to sign his pictures," according to the artifact's records. It was used by Tait to make his own picture frames, and it is currently stored in the Museum's collection with some of his other tools.

Arthur Fitzwilliam Tait was born in England in 1819, and he died in America in 1905, living most of his life in the New York City area and summering for many years in the Adirondack Mountains. His professional career spanned 55 years, and he was an enthusiastic sportsman.

Tait is best known for his nature scenes, especially during the time when 42 of his paintings were duplicated by lithographers Currier & Ives in the 1850s and '60s. The Adirondack Museum owns some of Tait's paintings, including "A Second Shot: Still Hunting on the First Snow in the Chateaugay Forest."

When Tait first arrived in the Adirondacks, he stayed at the Lake House on Lower Chateaugay Lake, according to Warder Cadbury's book "Arthur Fitzwilliam Tait: Artist in the Adirondacks." A room at the Lake House was put at his disposal to be used as a makeshift studio during stormy weather. In a short matter of time, Tait was exploring the Chateaugay Lakes by boat, looking for a place to create a camp of his own.

"This is the first shanty I ever built or lived in," the painter wrote on the reverse side of a crude oil sketch, "in the forest, built on Chateaugay Upper Lake, Franklin County, N.Y. on the west side in August, 1852. Painted from nature."

In the summer of 1855, Tait made his camp on the shores of Ragged Lake, a few miles southwest, near the mouth of a stream that is still called Tait Brook. This was the beginning of a slow move

A.F. Tait mould planer, artifact No. 57.137

(Photo courtesy of the Adirondack Museum)

southward to the central Adirondacks. As the mountains became more popular, and therefore more crowded, Tait sought solitude deeper and deeper in the woods.

In 1856, Tait began staying at a small boarding house at Loon Lake called Hunter's Home, which was operated by hotelier Apollos "Paul" Smith.

Notes made in 1858 prior to his camping trip reveal the art supplies needed for a summer season: "sketch box colours, sketching chair, canvas in a roll, solid sketch book & pencils, umbrella." He was soon camping with the Wardners on Bay Pond in the Rainbow Lake area.

In 1860, Tait decided to make his camp at Raquette Lake. The previous season, Smith had built a 17-bedroom hotel on the shore of Lower St. Regis Lake, the site of today's Paul Smith's College. The area "had become too developed to suit Tait's taste for shanty life," Cadbury wrote.

Tait stayed at Raquette Lake until 1869. That was the year William H. H. "Adirondack" Murray's best seller, "Adventures in the Wilderness," romanticized the Adirondack Mountains. His prose awakened the adventurous spirit of thousands, and hordes of middle- and upper-class tourists rushed to the Adirondacks, book in hand.

By 1870, Tait was summering at Palmer's boarding house in the Hamilton County hamlet of Long Lake. He then moved to South Pond, just 2 miles south of Palmer's.

By 1873, the painter had bought a 100-acre tract of land on the western shore of Long Lake, just below Clear Pond Stream and across from Mount Sabattis. When he arrived in Long Lake in the spring of 1874, he had decided to leave New York City for good and live in the Adirondacks year-round with his wife. His first son was born in 1875.

In the winter of 1877, Tait and his family began wintering again in New York City to avoid the coldest part of the year. By 1880, his wife, Polly, had died of childbed fever, shortly after their second son was born. By 1881, Tait decided to sell his Long Lake home and move back to New York City. He married Polly's sister, Emma, in the spring of 1882. She had helped take care of the children after her sister died.

Tait died in 1905, and although he sometimes said he wanted to be buried at the Long Lake Cemetery, he was interred at the Woodlawn Cemetery in Westchester County.

Chapter 9

Spruce gum boxes

If you are looking for a taste of the deep woods, literally a taste, then nothing beats a nugget of spruce gum. You could be in Times Square, trying to forget why you're in Times Square, and pop a drop of spruce gum in your mouth. Let it take you back to life on an Adirondack trail—to Ampersand Mountain, West Canada Lake or the Five Ponds Wilderness.

Sure, most people prefer the sweet sensation of maple syrup, but dried sap molded into a tiny morsel can give you hours of chewing time without losing its flavor. This is what Americans did before their grandchildren began throwing wads of Bubble Yum in their mouths during Little League baseball games. Maple syrup is made from the sugar maple tree, and spruce gum is preferably made from the red spruce. Either way, it boils down to this—sap is the taste of the deep woods.

While maple syrup production remains big business in the Northeast and city slickers pine for their Vermont maple products, the spruce gum trade—save for a few places—is a forgotten part of our economic history. It's only fresh in the minds of old-timers, historians and ethnobotanists.

Spruce gum manufacturing was an integral part of the Adirondack region's economy in the late 1800s and early 1900s. Two artifacts at the Adirondack Museum can attest to that: a pocket-sized box of Daniels Adirondack Spruce Gum (artifact No. 77.72) and a larger box of Smith's Celebrated Adirondack Spruce Gum (artifact No. 88.19). Both are currently in storage.

Daniels Adirondack Spruce Gum, "Prepared and distributed by Isaac Daniels Co. Poland, NY," was packaged in a beige box with a mountain scene and trees on the front. On the back and sides are instructions and promotional blurbs about spruce gum and its benefits. The box states that "Spruce Gum Sweetens the Breath" and "Spruce Gum Aids Digestion." It suggests that people let the gum warm in their mouths before chewing.

"This gum is used by doctors. It is recommended for throat, lung and stomach troubles. It is also used by dentists. It is recommended for maintaining healthy gums and preservation of the teeth."

The package, the size of a matchbox, held 12 drops and sold for 5 cents. "If you are unable to obtain this gum from your dealer, on

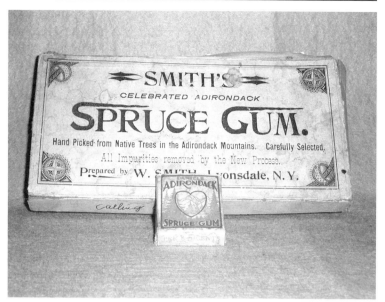

Spruce gum boxes, artifacts No. 88.19 (back) and 77.72.

(Photo courtesy of the Adirondack Museum)

receipt of $1.00 we will send you 20 of these 5 cent cartons; prepaid."
While the Daniels gum is currently not available, you can still buy
spruce gum, online, at $7.84 per ounce plus shipping.

Daniels began collecting spruce gum as a teenager just after the
Civil War, according to a 1993 Adirondack Life article by Elizabeth
Folwell. Originally from the Oneida County town of Boonville, he
later moved his business to Poland in Herkimer County and packaged
and wholesaled spruce gum until 1932, the year he died. The business
was then operated by his son for some years.

The prime months for harvesting spruce gum in the Adirondack
woods, March and April, are the same months that maple syrup is typically produced. Tree sap flows better on warm, sunny days after cold,
Adirondack nights.

Carrying a packbasket or a gunny sack and a gumming pole,
spruce gum collectors (a.k.a. gummers) looked for red spruce trees
with crystallized pitch from wounds on the bark. There was a cutter at
the end of the long wooden pole, and the chunks of pitch fell into a
cloth or metal receptacle a few inches down from the blade. Gummers
then put the sap into their baskets or sacks until they were full.

Back at the manufacturing plant, the sap was boiled in large cauldrons, skimmed and strained to remove the debris. Then it was poured into molds, wrapped in paper and packaged. Daniels created a process where the hot gum dripped off a metal plate and into cold water, creating uniform drops.

The Smith's Celebrated Adirondack Spruce Gum was "Hand Picked from Native Trees in the Adirondack Mountains." It was prepared by W. Smith, of Lyonsdale in Lewis County. The cardboard box with a hinged lid dates back to the 1920s. It was saved and used to store 5,200 Victorian calling cards by the person who donated them to the Munson-Williams-Proctor Institute in Utica. The calling cards dated from the mid-19th century to the early 20th century. The Institute kept the cards and donated the box to the Adirondack Museum.

People can make their own spruce gum by collecting the sap, boiling it until it's completely dissolved, and pouring it onto a greased cookie sheet.

The Fadden family at the Six Nations Indian Museum in Onchiota (Franklin County) used to make their own spruce gum and sell it to patrons. The children, who are all grown up now, were sent into the woods to collect the chunks of sap.

Native Americans introduced the custom of chewing spruce gum to the early North American settlers, according to the National Association of Chewing Gum Manufacturers. New Englanders created the first commercial chewing gum by selling and trading lumps of spruce. Spruce gum was popular until the 1850s, when paraffin wax became the new base for chewing gum.

Modern chewing gum products first appeared in 1869 after New York inventor Thomas Adams used chicle to produce his Adams New York No. 1 gum. Chicle- and latex-based gum soon became more popular than spruce or paraffin gum. It was smoother, softer and held its flavor better than any previous type of chewing gum. By the 1900s, chewing gum was manufactured in many different shapes, sizes and flavors, and bubble gum was invented in 1928 by Walter Diemer, a cost analyst for the Fleer Company.

Chapter 10

Carving bench

Even though woodcarving is traditionally a man's hobby, the grain of wood crossed gender lines years ago in the Adirondacks. Today women have secured a rightful seat in the court of Adirondack woodcarving. Women such as Karen Loffler, an amateur woodcarver in Saranac Lake who is leading the effort to build an Adirondack Carousel, are part of an international movement to express their creativity through wood. Groups like Women with Knives foster a sense of community among female carvers; they promote traditional carving techniques in quiet social settings while men's clubs meet in noisy, power-tool-buzzing rooms.

A century ago, women summering in the Adirondacks were hardly found in woodshops, bent over benches, shaping wood into fine art with chisels and gouges. Yet Mary Whitman Knauth, of New York City, spent countless hours in her Bolton Landing (Warren County) shop working on woodcarving projects in the early 1900s.

In 1988, the Adirondack Museum acquired a carving bench and tools used by Knauth. The table and tools are artifacts No. 88.71.1-34. They are currently in storage.

One of the Museum's curators wanted the woodcarving items for the collection "because it represents the leisure pursuits of upper middle class women in the Adirondacks."

The bench is an oak woodcarver's collapsible, trestle-style table. It has one drawer in the front, a wood-peg "work-dog" and pegs and wedges and braces. It is 38 inches tall, 33 inches wide and 23 inches deep.

Inside the drawer are woodworking tools. There are wood-handled chisels and gouges, an "India Stone" to sharpen the tools, wood-handled brushes with soft gray bristles, a broken ivory clamp, a clamp with wood jaws and a wood screw, a Lufkin folding rule No. 386, a folding crooked knife with a rosewood case, and a pine board level with a brass-plated steel edge and bubble intact.

The heavy bench was made largely of oak by Barker and Robinson (B&R) about 1905. B&R had a small shop at the bottom of the hill at Bolton's Landing on Lake George, where the Knauth house stands. The shop and the Knauth's Waldeck camp shared Artist's Brook, which ran alongside the buildings. B&R used the brook for power, having a waterwheel to run all their equipment.

Carving bench and tools, artifacts No. 88.71.1-34

(Photo courtesy of the Adirondack Museum)

Artist's Brook also gave electricity to Waldeck. It had the first electric power on Lake George and charged the batteries for the Barbara, the electric boat that took the Knauths around Lake George at 6 mph. Waldeck, which means "corner of the wood," was built by Knauth's husband about 1900.

The Knauths' granddaughter donated the carving bench and tools to the Adirondack Museum. In her correspondence with a curator, she said that her father remembered when the oak table arrived at the Bolton Landing house when he was a boy.

Mary Whitman Knauth was born in 1861 in Massachusetts and married Percival Knauth in 1883 or 1884. He worked at a German bank in New York City. She had five sons, the youngest of whom was the donor's father (one of twins).

The Museum's collection includes a few other items once owned by Mary Whitman Knauth: an oak board bookstand with carved bookends mortised into each end and a black dress bodice of silk net over satin, trimmed with black beads. Knauth carved the bookcase and bookends at Waldeck. The carving bench was always at Waldeck, not in New York City, where the Knauths lived in the winter.

Chapter 11

Freshwater pearl stick pin

Adirondackers know it is spring when tubs of night crawlers begin appearing next to the 2 percent milk in convenience store refrigerators. M.C. Rowe didn't have that luxury in 1892, but his search for fishing bait in a St. Lawrence County brook led to the rare discovery of freshwater pearls.

Some of these pearls were made into jewelry, and the Adirondack Museum owns a gold stick pin (artifact No. 77.60) with 21 tiny pearls harvested from those very waters.

Rowe, a spruce-gum manufacturer, was fishing in Frost Brook, a tributary of the Grass River near Russell. He ran out of bait and opened a mussel or freshwater clam. Inside he found a pink pearl the size of a pea. Rowe soon gave up the spruce gum business and focused his attention on pearl fishing.

"Using long poles with pinchers and boxes with glass for spying the mollusks partially buried in the sand, he and over 80 men and boys from nearby Russell hauled mussels up by the thousands until the surrounding creeks and river eventually became depleted," noted a 1986 "Speaking Artifactually" article in the Museum's newsletter.

The piles of decaying river mussels created a bad odor; therefore, town officials required fishermen to open up the mollusks at their own homes. Rowe and others hired gatherers, who sold the pearls to Tiffany's and diamond merchants.

The St. Lawrence Plain Dealer reported on the local pearl business in the 1890s: "The pearl fisheries at Russell are the scenes of busy operations these days, and many handsome pearls are found. Fifteen bushels of clams are sometimes opened by one person. Various stories are told of the value of some of the pearls found, but $125 is probably the highest cash price paid for any single pearl."

For the next couple of years, the town of Russell enjoyed a thriving business in freshwater pearls, but in 1894 the supply was nearly exhausted. The same thing happened in the 1850s during the American Pearl Rush.

The Pearl Rush began in 1857 in a New Jersey stream, where a pearl found in a mussel was eventually sold by Tiffany's for $2,500, according to G. Thomas Watters, of the Ohio Biological Survey and the Ohio State University Aquatic Ecology Laboratory. The U.S. Geological Survey (USGS) differs on the location of the find, stating

Stick pin, artifact No. 77.60, made from freshwater pearls found in the St. Lawrence County town of Russell

(Photo courtesy of the Adirondack Museum)

Ohio as the source, but both agree that the Pearl Rush led to the killing of hundreds of thousands of mussels throughout the U.S. in pursuit of freshwater pearls.

Soon after the Pearl Rush, entrepreneurs were harvesting mussels for mother-of-pearl shells to use in the button-making industry. Now these mollusks are used for the cultured pearl industry, where pieces of mussel shell are inserted into pearl oysters and used as nuclei to start the pearl-making process.

Freshwater native clams are now the most endangered animal group in North America, according to the USGS.

Pearl buyers continued to visit Russell at least once a year after the St. Lawrence County Pearl Rush was over. From 1915 to 1920, Floyd Conant regularly drove a buyer, allegedly from Tiffany's, from the railroad station at DeKalb to Russell. On his last trip, the buyer gave Conant the gold stick pin set with Grass River pearls as a memento. The pin eventually passed into the hands of Conant's brother, Leland Conant, who, with his wife, presented it to the Adirondack Museum in April 1977.

On the stick pin, eight petals are arranged around the center of the "flower" that makes the pin-head. The petals each have two or three pearls with a single pearl (no larger than a sesame seed) with a bluish hue at the center. The petals form a spiral one-fourth inch in diameter, about the size of a person's fingernail. The pin is 2.25 inches long. Any mollusk that produces a shell can produce a pearl. Naturally occurring pearls are rare, found in one of every 10,000 animals, according to the American Museum of Natural History.

Chapter 12

Echo Camp store

Memories of summer camp at 4-H Camp Overlook in northern Franklin County reverberate in my mind as happy highlights of my childhood.

For seven years, starting at age 8, I spent at least one week each summer with my 4-H buddies boating, swimming, shooting BBs and arrows at targets, and singing around campfires at dusk. It was the first time away from home, the first time I danced with girls and the first time I actually looked forward to going to the store—the camp store, that is.

After lunch every day, we'd run to the back to the main lodge, where the camp store was brimming with candy, combs, paper and pens. There were postcards to fill out and teeth to brush during the post-lunch rest period, yet I was content just sitting on my cabin bunk gnawing on strawberry taffy or a Charleston Chew. For many campers, time spent at the camp store was a treat. After all, the money they spent belonged to their parents.

Starting on May 24, the Adirondack Museum will begin celebrating the history of children's camps when it opens a two-year exhibit, "A Paradise for Boys and Girls: Children's Camps in the Adirondacks." I'm not sure if they'll have any artifacts from Camp Overlook in Mountain View, but one fascinating item on display will be the Echo Camp store used at this former girls camp on Raquette Lake.

The Echo Camp store, artifact No. 2002.7, is a large box that sits on a single axle with two large wagon wheels. The entire cart, 26 inches tall and 52 inches wide, is painted red and yellow. There is a heavy, removable lid and cubbies inside for merchandise. The store, which sold pens, pencils, stationery, postcards and souvenirs to campers, lived on the porch of Echo Camp's Lounsbury cabin, known by the girls as "Skipper's Cabin."

Skipper was the camp name of its founder, director and owner, Frances Clough Havinga. She donated the artifact to the Museum in 2002. Echo Camp was her life and love, according to her son, Carl Clough, who had worked at the camp during his high school and college years.

The camp store was made by Mrs. Havinga's daughter, Jean Clough Martino, and her husband, Jack. They constructed it in North

Echo Camp store, artifact No. 2002.7

(Photo courtesy of the Adirondack Museum)

Carolina and transported it to Raquette Lake on their station wagon. That was about 40 years ago, according to Museum records.

The store opened for business several days a week after lunch and before the mandatory daily rest period. It included candy, film, postcards, writing paper, toothpaste, combs, pencils, etc. There was no chewing gum; that was strictly forbidden, according to her son. Campers had cash accounts, which were set up by their parents, for store purchases.

Echo Camp on Raquette Lake's Long Point was originally built for Phineas Lounsbury starting in 1880. A Civil War veteran, Lounsbury was a member of the Connecticut House of Representatives in the 1870s and the governor of Connecticut from 1887 to 1889. Several generations of Lounsburys vacationed at Echo Camp until it was sold in 1948 to Mrs. Havinga, who ran it as the Echo Camp for Girls until she retired in the mid-1980s. The Great Camp was added to the National Register of Historic Places in 1986. It is now used as a private family estate.

The Museum's exhibit, "A Paradise for Boys and Girls: Children's Camps in the Adirondacks," will explore the impact of camps on the region's economy, the aims of camp directors and counselors, and the ways in which the camp experience has molded the lives of the campers. It will include subtitles such as "The Waterfront," "Campers as Consumers," "Camping and the Adirondack Environment" and "Camp Gatherings." The exhibit's curator is Hallie Bond.

"Viewed within the context of camping nationwide, Adirondack camps have been relatively homogeneous and expensive," Bond wrote in the exhibit's description. "Even so, a diverse group of camps has existed in the region. Camps established for Jewish children, for special needs children, camps set up by YMCAs, the Catholic Church, 4-H and the Conservation Department have all tried to teach their own values."

The first children's camp in the Adirondack Mountains was the YMCA's Camp Dudley, which moved to Lake Champlain in 1891. More than 320 camps have existed in the region since that time.

Chapter 13

Jacob Asanger painting

Art and tourism were married in the Adirondacks in the mid-1800s. Mother Nature conducted the ceremony in a remote location, using an easel as an altar and a pine grove as a chapel. The honeymoon has never ended.

Once the painted beauty of the mountains reached the eyes of East Coast city dwellers, they were compelled to witness the natural beauty of New York's unspoiled wilderness for themselves.

Thanks to Thomas Cole and other members of the famed Hudson River School of landscape painting, artists traveled north and found the pristine Adirondacks a favorite place to sit and paint. Cole, for example, painted "Schroon Lake" in 1846. Artists such as Arthur Fitzwilliam Tait were soon depicting scenes from Adirondack woods and waters, and lithographers at Currier & Ives were mass producing copies of these paintings for public consumption.

The writings of William H.H. "Adirondack" Murray convinced droves of middle-class residents to visit the Adirondacks after the Civil War.

"It is a paradise, and so will it continue to be while a deer leaves his track upon the shores of its lakes or a trout shows himself above the surface of its waters," Murray wrote in his 1869 best seller, "Adventures in the Wilderness."

Yet it was the painting community that ultimately gave would-be tourists a glimpse of what they were about to see.

A new exhibit at the Adirondack Museum, "Summering in the Adirondacks: The Artists' Views," will feature paintings and artifacts from summer destinations, including the High Peaks, Lake George and Ausable Chasm. The exhibit's cover painting, "Adirondack Mountains, New York," by Jacob Asanger, is fitting because it was commissioned specifically to be reproduced as a poster to lure tourists to the Adirondack Park. It is artifact No. 2002.66 in the Museum's collection.

"It's a wonderful example of art and tourism and traveling, a joint effort of art and commerce," said Caroline Welsh, chief curator and director of operations at the Adirondack Museum. "It says, 'This is a beautiful place.'"

The landscape is oil on canvas, a typical 4-by-4-foot Asanger painting. It depicts a scene with water in the foreground, a birch tree and shrubbery in the middle ground and a red-roofed barn or house

Jacob Asanger painting, "Adirondack Mountains, New York," artifact No. 2002.66

(Photo courtesy of the Adirondack Museum)

hidden in front of blue and green mountains and a clouded sky in the background. He painted it in 1920.

Asanger was born in Altotting, Bavaria in 1887, and his family moved to the United States in the late 1800s, settling in Los Angeles. During his career, he was a portrait and landscape painter, poster artist, etcher, craftsman and art teacher. He lived in California, Montana and New York and taught at the Chouinard Art School in Los Angeles until his death in 1941, according to "Who Was Who in American Art."

The Los Angeles advertising firm Foster and Kleiser hired Asanger to paint landscapes around the United States, and the company reproduced the paintings as posters to promote tourist destinations. In addition to the Adirondacks, he had visited and painted famous American landmarks such as Old Faithful in Yellowstone National Park and the Garden of the Gods at Colorado Springs, Colo. Asanger set up a studio in New York City in the 1910s, allowing him to paint on the East Coast and in the Adirondacks.

The "Summering in the Adirondacks" exhibit will be open from May 23 to Oct. 13 in the Lynn H. Boillot Art Galleries at the Adirondack Museum. It will include images and artifacts of summer pastimes: boating, fishing, camping and places to go and stay. It will feature masterworks from the Museum's renowned painting collection, and the message is clear: artwork is an integral player in the Adirondack tourism industry.

While not specifically designed as commercial art, the landscapes of contemporary Adirondack painters such as Tim Fortune and Matt Burnett in Saranac Lake continue to inspire our imagination and excite our sense of adventure, luring us to a misty Saranac River at dawn or a backcountry lean-to on the Northville-Placid Trail. They remind us that romance can still be found in the Adirondack Mountains.

Chapter 14

Children's camp war canoe

Today's war canoes are a far cry from those used in battles on Lake Champlain during the American Revolution. Instead of bows, arrows and war paint, Adirondack "paddle battle" gear tops the list with smelly bug dope, green head nets and orange life jackets. Maybe some bubble gum and a digital camera.

One war canoe on exhibit at the Adirondack Museum, artifact No. 99.8, is covered with green-painted canvas, not birch bark as it would have been more than 200 years ago. It was purchased in 1941 for the Schroon Lake girls summer camp, Camp Nawita, in Essex County. It was later sold to a nearby boys camp on Paradox Lake.

This artifact is significant for two reasons. It reminds us of the history of non-motorized boating in the Adirondacks, which will be celebrated from June 13 to 15 during the annual No-Octane Regatta on Blue Mountain Lake. It also symbolizes the waterfront activities at summer camps.

The canoe is featured in the Museum's "Boats and Boating in the Adirondacks" building to help celebrate the new exhibit, "A Paradise for Boys and Girls: Children's Camps in the Adirondacks."

The contemporary war canoe was established in Canada in the late 1800s.

"War canoes, open paddling canoes 25 to 35 feet long, first became popular in the 1870s among canoe clubs in Canada as a way for members who couldn't afford their own canoe to enjoy paddling in a group," wrote the Museum's Hallie Bond, curator of "A Paradise for Boys and Girls," in the artifact's file.

An 1890 article in Forest and Stream magazine featured the Ko-Ko-Ko-Ho war canoe with a description and design drawings given with permission of the designers and builders, the St. Lawrence River Skiff, Canoe and Steam Launch Co., of Clayton.

"We thought when the 'girling canoe' was finally christened a couple of years ago that the demands of every class of canoeist were fully provided for," stated the article, "but each new season seems to bring its particular specialty, and as 1888 and Lake George will always be remembered as a great year of the dude and the open canoe, so 1889 will be marked in canoe history as the date of another novel feature in canoeing."

The first war canoe was devised by the Toronto C.C. and built by

Nawita war canoe, artifact No. 99.8, before it was placed on exhibit

(Photo courtesy of the Adirondack Museum)

the Ontario Canoe Co. for them, according to Forest and Stream. The Unktahee was a huge craft, 30 ft. long, manned by 16 paddlers and a steersman, and the cargo consisted of "pretty girls without number, who were carried off only too willingly by the professional beauties of the Toronto C.C."

The early war canoes were of all-wood construction. After 1900, they were built with wood-canvas technology and became popular at children's camps. The 25-foot war canoes, such as the Nawita, were generally paddled by crews of six to 10.

The Nawita was built by the Old Town Company in Old Town, Maine. A Schroon Lake man who had purchased Camp Paradox on Paradox Lake in the 1970s donated it to the Adirondack Museum in 1999.

Established in 1910, Camp Paradox featured activities such as camping trips, nature study, sports and dramatics. A 1930 advertisement for the camp stated that the facility was for boys 8-18 years of age. There were 95 kids enrolled, with a staff of 15, and the cost was $400 for the season. Camp Paradox was a boys camp until the late 1950s or early 1960s and then closed briefly. It reopened for one year, serving boys and girls, and then closed permanently.

Polaroid pictures of the Nawita canoe reveal that the craft was stored in a dirty shed or garage before it was donated. It was leaning against an insulation-lined wall on its side with a black plastic bag in the middle. Strewn around the canoe were metal bed frames, a roll of chain-link fencing, loose yellow insulation, empty clear plastic bags, cardboard boxes stuffed with junk, and a blue-and-white plastic kick ball. The canoe was well used and aging; the paint was faded to a light aqua green color and peeling so much that it looked like the pattern of a turtle shell. After the donation, the canvas piece was taken off the canoe and restored to its original dark green color, with the word Nawita painted on the front with gold and red letters.

In 1940, the cost of this canoe was $135. It was stocked in green and could be ordered in red, orange and yellow.

In a 1947 Old Town advertisement, we see why so many children's camps purchased these canoes for their waterfront programs: "Boys' and girls' summer camps and canoe clubs use this canoe for team paddling and group cruising. No watercraft is better for team training. It is a pretty sight to see a War canoe driving with rhythmic strokes at top speed."

Chapter 15

'Places of the Spirit' photo, Chapel Island

Sitting on a mound of rock, an island barely an acre in size, is a sacred site. A tiny brown chapel, hugged by pine trees, seems to float on a holy barge anchored in the azure blue waters of Upper Saranac Lake.

With sunlight glittering on the ripples, a loon wailing in the distance, pine needles baking in the summer heat, and a soft breeze cooling speckles of sweat on your neck, it soon hits.

This is God's country.

The Island Chapel, a bona fide place of spirit, serves residents and visitors with non-denominational services every Sunday morning in the summertime. It is an Upper Saranac Lake institution, a tourist destination and a popular wedding venue. Instead of a neon sign, a 12-foot-tall birch tree cross lures boaters to its rocky shore, strewn with green lichen, amber pine needles and driftwood. For many people, it is heaven on Earth, or at least a symbol of it.

This chapel, located in Franklin County, is featured in the "Places of Spirit: Sacred Sites of the Adirondacks" traveling exhibit currently on display at the Adirondack Museum. The show and accompanying book, produced by the Lake Placid Institute for the Arts and Humanities, is designed to look "deeply, through the lenses of four contemporary photographers, at structures and landscapes in the Adirondack region of New York that signify or once signified spiritual use and meaning."

Romaine Orthwein's photograph, "Chapel Island," captures the essence of the site. The viewer's eye is drawn to the contrast of a woman in a white dress walking toward the brown-stained chapel (we see her back). To the right is the birch-log cross. Under her bare feet is solid rock. To the left are blueberry bushes, shrubs and a white pine sapling at the foot of a towering Scotch pine tree. Above are cirrocumulus clouds flying high in a blue sky. The woman in the white dress is the photographer.

Orthwein has another Chapel Island photo in the "Places of Spirit" book; this time, her camera, placed inside the chapel, looks out large glass windows to the rocky shore of the island, the light gray waters of Upper Saranac Lake and the forested western shoreline. Again, the photographer is dressed in white in the photograph, squatting on the lakeshore, dipping her fingers in the cool lake water.

The first chapel on the island was built in 1889 in the Victorian style. In 1892, the same year New York state formed the Adirondack Park, three Plattsburgh attorneys gave the island to the Champlain Presbytery.

Lumberjack sky pilot Aaron Maddox served as the first minister for this chapel and the Indian Carry Chapel. After the original structure was razed by fire in 1956, it was rebuilt in 1958 with Adirondack siding and a foundation of stone masonry.

Access to Chapel Island is limited to boaters only. A party boat transports parishioners from nearby Indian Carry to the island. Lake residents drive their motorboats to the island and anchor them in a floating parking lot; they are taken to shore by a designated chauffeur. People in guideboats and canoes may tie their crafts to the dock, though it can get crowded when the shuttle arrives.

The "Places of Spirit" exhibit includes framed images from Orthwein, Shellburne Thurber, Barry Lobdell and Heather McLeod. The Lake Placid Institute commissioned them to shoot photographs of their own choosing that conveyed a sense of the spiritual or sacred.

"In many instances, the structures remain a vital part of Adirondack communities and are used on a regular basis as sites of worship or village life," said Jennifer Carlo, executive director of the Lake Placid Institute.

The exhibit includes pictures of St. Brendan's Roman Catholic Church in Keene, the Beth-Joseph Synagogue in Tupper Lake, and St. Christopher's Church in North Creek.

Some of these sacred buildings have been adapted to new uses. The Essex Senior Center was formerly the Methodist Episcopal Church in Essex, built in 1835. An Orvis store in Wevertown had once been the Methodist Church.

"Other special places where the spiritual resides are the private chapels or personal religious spaces that Adirondackers have built into their home or camps," Carlo said. "And lastly, there is the landscape itself—pieces of hillsides that have been made into graveyards and cemeteries, and then the larger landscape, the mountaintops and slopes and the waters of Adirondack lakes and rivers."

The "Places of the Spirit" exhibit is curated by Mara Miller, an independent curator from New York. It will be on display in Blue Mountain Lake through Oct. 13 and will then travel to the Housatonic Museum of Art in Bridgeport, Conn. The book is available in regional bookstores or by calling the Lake Placid Institute at (518) 523-1312 or logging on to its Web site at www.lakeplacidinstitute.org.

The Lake Placid Institute was founded in 1994 and is dedicated to nurturing the arts in upstate New York and the Adirondacks with a target audience in the High Peaks region surrounding the village of Lake Placid. The Institute sponsors international music seminars, the Adirondack Roundtable discussions, the annual Words From the Woods poetry contest for Adirondack children, the New Dramatists program for New York City playwrights visiting the mountains, leadership and ethical fitness seminars and the World of Children's Literature two-day seminar every fall in Lake Placid.

Chapter 16

Rushton Saranac Laker guideboat

One of the Adirondack Museum's guideboats has traveled hundreds of miles in more than 30 years, yet it hasn't touched the water in all that time.

This watercraft—a Saranac Laker guideboat built by J. Henry Rushton's company in the St. Lawrence County village of Canton—is currently on display at the Adirondack Museum Store on Main Street in Lake Placid. It is artifact No. 69.180 in the Museum's collection. The boat was donated in 1969 by a woman who had it at her Brant Lake camp. That is presumably where the craft was used.

Since then, it has been loaned to several organizations throughout New York state. It was on display at the Thousand Islands Shipyard Museum in Clayton in the 1970s and early 1980s. The St. Lawrence County Historical Association featured the boat at its Canton headquarters in 1988 and 1989. It was displayed at the Buffalo Society of Natural Sciences/Buffalo Museum of Science in 1994. And it spent time at Syracuse University's Minnowbrook Conference Center in Blue Mountain Lake in the late 1990s.

After being loaned to so many places, the guideboat was in need of attention and was recently restored, fittingly, by a boat builder/restorer in Canton.

It is not clear from the Adirondack Museum's records when this Saranac Laker was constructed, yet there is no doubt who built it—the master himself. It can simply be called a Rushton boat, and jaws will drop out of respect.

"If boats lasted as long as violins and were cherished as much, (Rushton) might become the Stradivarius of the canoe," Atwood Manley wrote in his "Rushton and His Times in American Canoeing" book. "Now that a few of his craft are preserved in museums, the possibility cannot be ruled out."

Rushton was born in 1843 south of the village of Edwards in St. Lawrence County. He moved to Canton in his late 20s and settled down as a boat builder, making canoes, guideboats, skiffs, rowboats and other types of small watercraft.

Rushton first introduced his Saranac Laker guideboat in his 1888 catalog in 15- and 16-foot models. In 1891, he reduced his offering to only a 16-foot boat, yet in 1895 he was offering to make versions of the craft in lengths up to 20 feet upon special order. The Museum's

Saranac Laker guideboat, artifact No. 69.180, on exhibit in Lake Placid
(Photo courtesy of the Adirondack Museum)

Saranac Laker is 15 feet, 10 inches long.

The early Rushton guideboats, 1888 to 1890, seem to have solid seats, a square gunwale strip and rib spacing of 6 to 7 inches, according to the Museum's records. A former curator noted that Rushton went to caned seats and a rounded gunwale strip about 1891. Sometime between that date and 1903, Rushton reduced the rib spacing to 4 inches. In 1903, he was offering to build the Saranac Laker with steam-bent as well as sawn ribs.

The Saranac Laker was Rushton's only version of the guideboat. He made the craft out of demand; his passion was building canoes. A former Adirondack Museum curator speculated, "Rushton never really enjoyed making guideboats." That's because his basic canoe construction technique (small, steam-bent ribs, closely spaced together) was at odds with the sawn ribs of the traditional Adirondack guideboat. This may have explained Rushton's gradual shortening of the rib spacing and the option of steam-bent ribs for the Saranac Laker.

"The canoe was his mousetrap," Manley wrote. "First the local people, then the world made a beaten path to the door of his boat shop in the village of Canton."

Canoes with names such as the Kleiner Fritz, Sairy Gamp and

Aurora Vesper were written about regularly in leading sporting journals during Rushton's career. He was one of 23 people who founded the American Canoe Association. Rushton died in 1906 at the age of 62 and was buried in the Fairview Cemetery in Canton.

Those interested in canoes, guideboats and other Adirondack watercraft may find the No-Octane Regatta interesting. It will be held this weekend in Blue Mountain Lake and will include wooden boat races, a Grand Parade of Boats, demonstrations and workshops.

Chapter 17

Adirondack Railroad 1892 silver spike

When Louis Jordan recorded the jazz classic "Choo Choo Ch'Boogie" in 1946, the New York Central's Adirondack Division was still in its prime.

"I love to hear the rhythm of the clickety clack, and hear the lonesome whistle, see the smoke from the stack."

By the time Asleep at the Wheel recorded its western swing version of the song in 1974, the tracks between Utica and Lake Placid were abandoned and silent. That's the same year Adirondack Museum curators learned they would be receiving a silver spike from the railroad's 1892 opening ceremony. The spike is artifact No. 74.82.1 in the Museum's collection (currently in storage).

The spike was given to the donors' great-grandfather, John Black Sr., when the railroad line between Remsen and Malone was completed. It was owned by his son, John H. Black Jr., until his death. John H. Black Jr.'s grandson and granddaughter gave it to the Museum "in his memory and in the keeping of the history of the Adirondacks."

John Black Sr., also known as Judge Black because he was a justice of the peace in the Tupper Lake Junction, owed his railroading success to a bottle of liquor.

"I claim that a bottle of Pepper whiskey was responsible for my success with the New York Central Railroad," Black said in a 1922 newspaper interview with the Utica Observer-Dispatch.

"To Judge Black perhaps more than any other living man today with the exception of Dr. Seward Webb, is due the credit for much of the construction of the Adirondack Division," the article stated.

In 1890, Dr. William Seward Webb financed a railroad that would pass through his hunting preserve, Nehasane Park, on Lake Lila. His line was initially built from Herkimer to Malone and finally to Montreal. It became part of the New York Central System in 1893 and has been known by several names over the years: the Mohawk and Malone Railway, Adirondack & St. Lawrence Line, NYC Adirondack Division line and simply the Adirondack Railroad (although Dr. Thomas Durant's line to North Creek, finished in 1871, was originally called the Adirondack Railroad).

Black was one of the earliest contractors for Webb's railroad, making his way to Tupper Lake in heavy snow during the severe winter of 1888. He had a few teams and was looking for "the best job" he

Silver spike, artifact No. 74.82.1, owned by Tupper Lake Judge John Black Sr.

(Photo courtesy of the Adirondack Museum)

could get. John Hurd, one of the railroad/logging pioneers in the Tupper Lake region, introduced him to Webb and his chief engineer, Norman Roberts.

Black said he had traveled from Plattsburgh and would wait for the railroad work to begin. In the meantime, he helped out with surveying and odd jobs. While he was acting as flagman for the surveyor, Roberts became sick, and Black gave him a bottle of Pepper whiskey for his illness.

"The following morning, cured, he came to me," Black told the Observer-Dispatch.

Roberts thanked Black for the whiskey and asked him about his railroad-building experience. Black explained that his last position was on the Memorie and Maderia Railroad in Brazil.

"Immediately he said that I was the man he needed, and from that time on I was Superintendent of Right of Way Improvement," Black said.

As the song goes, "Gonna settle down by the railroad track, live the life of Riley in a beaten-down shack."

Black did settle down, eventually, in Tupper Lake. As the construction supervisor, his territory extended from Remsen to Malone. Before the tracks were laid, he traveled by foot and horses and claimed that he had once walked from Malone to Remsen in only two weeks, checking up on contractors and estimating their progress.

This was only 20 years after the Transcontinental Railroad across the United States had been constructed. The Union Pacific Railroad laid tracks west from Omaha, Neb., and the Central Pacific Railroad laid them east from Sacramento, Calif. They met in Promontory, Utah and celebrated with a Golden Spike Ceremony on May 10, 1869.

The Adirondack rails were laid north from Remsen and south from Malone. The junction of the lines was at Twitchell Creek south of Beaver River.

On the day that the rails were joined, a gala celebration was held, according to the 1922 article. Silver-plated spikes were used in laying the last rail, and one was given to Black as a souvenir. The spike is engraved with the words, "Dilworth, Porter & Co. Lt'l, Pittsburgh, Pa. Goldie Pat'd Perfect RR Spike."

The date was Oct. 12, 1892. Knowing this was an historic occasion, the judge also saved two of the rolls that were served at a dinner honoring the railroad employees. For his achievements, the railroad company gave Black a 200-acre farm, 6 miles from Malone, which he had still owned in 1922.

The first train from Herkimer to Thendara ran on July 1, 1892, and the first train from New York City to Montreal ran on Oct. 24, 1892, according to a history written by Adirondack Scenic Railroad's Linda Ellison.

Today, we know the Adirondack Railroad, or Adirondack Scenic Railroad, as a Utica to Lake Placid line. The tracks from Lake Clear to Malone were abandoned in 1961, and scheduled passenger service from Utica to Lake Placid was discontinued in 1965. In 1968, the New York Central System merged with the Pennsylvania Railroad and became the Penn Central Transportation Company. Freight service ended in 1972.

New York state purchased the tracks in 1975 and leased them to the Adirondack Railway Corporation from 1977 to 1981 so people could be transported from Utica to Lake Placid for the 1980 Olympic Winter Games. The tracks were abandoned a year later.

In 1992 and 1993, a group of railway enthusiasts operated the 4-mile Adirondack Centennial Railroad from Thendara south to Minnehaha. In 1994, the excursion line became the Adirondack Scenic Railroad, operated by the Adirondack Railway Preservation Society.

By the year 2000, the railroad tracks were restored south to Snow Junction (which is connected to Utica by freight tracks), 6 miles north from Thendara to Carter Station, and 11 miles between Saranac Lake and Lake Placid. Excursion lines now run from May to October in those regions, and visitors continue to enjoy their own "Choo Choo Ch'Boogie" through the beautiful Adirondack Mountains.

"I just love the rhythm of the clickety clack, so, take me right back to the track, Jack!"

Chapter 18

Old Mountain Phelps packbasket

In 1876, legendary Glens Falls photographer Seneca Ray Stoddard captured the image of a bona fide mountain man living in the Adirondack High Peaks region, packbasket and all.

Orson Schofield Phelps, also known as Old Mountain Phelps, was a legend in his own right—woodsman, hunter, trapper, fisherman, poet, philosopher and backwoods guide. And when he wasn't on a "random scoot" to Mount Marcy, he even made packbaskets.

In 1956, a Keene Valley resident donated a packbasket to the Adirondack Museum, one that Phelps had made for Mrs. Charles A. Goodwin, of Hartford, Conn. It is artifact No. 56.42 in the Museum's collection and is currently in storage. (The Museum also has the Stoddard picture of Phelps from Sept. 27, 1876 in its Historic Photo Collection.)

There's not much information available about the packbasket, only that it is a round mouth subtype with ash splints. Phelps, though, was fascinating enough to be featured in several history books since he roamed the woods in the late 1800s.

"I think that Old Mountain Phelps had merely the instincts of the primitive man, and never any hostile civilizing intent as to the wilderness into which he plunged," wrote Charles Dudley Warner in his 1878 book, "In the Wilderness," reprinted by the Adirondack Museum and Syracuse University Press.

"He was a true citizen of the wilderness," Warner continued. "[Henry David] Thoreau would have liked him, as he liked Indians and woodchucks, and the smell of pine-forests. And if Old Phelps had seen Thoreau, he would probably have said to him, 'Why on airth, Mr. Thoreau, don't you live accordin' to your preachin'?'"

In his character study of Phelps, Warner called him "a real son of the soil" and tells stories about the guide's grooming practices, as well as his relationship with and attitude toward soap.

"Soap is a thing," Phelps said in a "small, high-pitched, querulous" voice, "that I hain't no kinder use for."

Warner admired the old guide's knowledge of the backcountry and his excellent woodcraft, dedicating a whole chapter to this man's unique qualities. "One does not think of Old Phelps so much as a lover of nature—to use the sentimental slang of the period—as a part of nature itself."

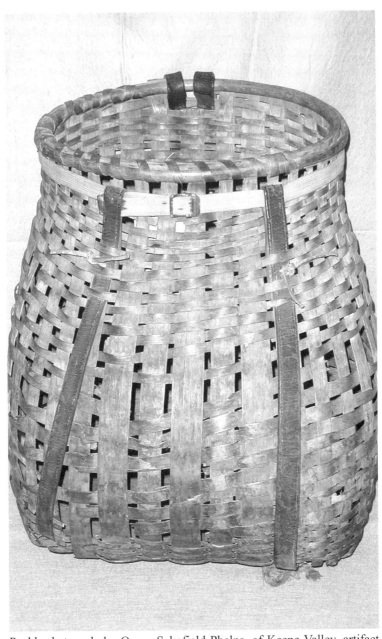

Packbasket made by Orson Schofield Phelps, of Keene Valley, artifact No. 56.42

(Photo courtesy of the Adirondack Museum)

Phelps was born on May 6, 1816 in Vermont and moved to the Schroon Lake region in Essex County around 1830. His birth year has been misprinted as 1817 in some history books; however, his obituary in the Utica Post-Dispatch and the "Genealogy of Orson Schofield Phelps Family" states 1816 as the year of birth. All sources agree that the day was May 6.

Phelps worked at the Adirondack Iron Works in the town of Newcomb when hiring began in 1832, according to Bill Healy's book, "The High Peaks of Essex: The Adirondack Mountains of Orson Schofield Phelps." But he left after the tragic death of Iron Works manager David Henderson in 1845 at what is now known as Calamity Pond.

Alfred Donaldson, in "The History of the Adirondacks," wrote that Phelps was the carpenter of the town's schoolhouse in 1850. The guide lived on Clough Brook and operated a sawmill, Phelps told the New York State Canal Board in 1858. He established the first postal service in Keen Flats, now Keene Valley, in 1865, carrying mail for six months until the government took over. He also had lumbering and coopering accounts, and we know he made packbaskets, but he was better known for being a real deal Adirondack guide. He was even immortalized by Winslow Homer when the famous 19th century painter portrayed Phelps and fellow guide Harvey Holt in his "Two Guides" painting.

Phelps died at his Keene Valley home on April 14, 1905 at the age of 88. As long as the state Legislature doesn't begin renaming the 46 High Peaks for loyal politicians, we will always remember the name of Old Mountain Phelps. As a fitting tribute to a true mountain man, Mount Phelps, at 4,161 feet, stands roughly between Mount Marcy and the Adirondak Loj and is the 32nd highest peak in New York state.

While literate, Phelps did not regard himself as a literary genius, yet he was an avid reader of Horace Greeley's Tribune and wrote regularly for the Essex County Republican. He even sketched maps of the Keene Valley area and wrote a booklet, "The Growth of a Tree: From its Germ or Seed," for the Essex County Republican. It is 26 pages long and includes the poem, "Autumn Leaves."

At the end of the booklet, Phelps recorded a "Note to the Public" disclaimer: "The author of this little work does not make any pretensions to literary merit, and hence may not be able to please the critic; but anyone who loves nature and all that she teaches, will find pleasure in the observations of one who has been a life long student of nature in her original language."

Chapter 19

Northville 1859 Fourth of July poster

Normally when I write about an artifact for the "Adirondack Attic," I have an accession file with historical tidbits to lead me on a time-travel journey. During the research process, the information collectively blossoms into a flower of human history, with each petal taking me on a unique side trip—to a book, a person, a Web site.

This week's Adirondack Museum artifact, a Fourth of July celebration poster from Northville in 1859, was an accession file in itself. The poster had no accompanying documentation and left me with the question, "What am I going to write about?"

After a few weeks of the "don't worry, be happy" mentality, it was time to write the column, and I accepted the challenge with zeal.

The solution: Have fun with history. After all, one of the most gratifying perks of this job is discovering people's connections to each other and to places in the Adirondack region. So I decided to answer the question, "What's in a poster?"

First of all, I had to get the poster's date correct. The 5 in "NORTHVILLE, JUNE 27, 1859" looks like a 3, so I thought the date was 1839. After adding 83, from the "Eighty Third Anniversary of our National Independence," to 1776, I concluded that 1859 was the correct date.

Other information on the poster, namely the guest orator and the 33 female stars of the day, supported the fact that this ceremony was held in 1859.

"Thirty-three juvenile ladies will represent the States, and form in procession with the adult ladies, to whom a suitable place in the Procession will be assigned," the poster stated.

On Feb. 14, 1859, Oregon became the 33rd state in the Union. At the time, the United States was flying the 32-star flag, which became official on July 4, 1858, less than two months after Minnesota became the 32nd state. The 33-star flag became official on July 4, 1859 and was used for two years, under U.S. presidents James Buchanan and Abraham Lincoln. The 34-star flag became official on July 4, 1861 after Kansas became the 34th state.

The 1859 Fourth of July ceremony in Northville was held on June 27. This was a busy and historic time around the world. Ground was broken on the Suez Canal two months earlier. In two weeks, Charles Dickens would publish "A Tale of Two Cities." By the end of the sum-

FOURTH

OF JULY.

Eighty Third Anniversary
OF OUR NATIONAL INDEPENDENCE.

Will be celebrated at Northville, in accordance with that spirit which should actuate every lover of his country, and the Committee of Arrangements give a cordial invitation to all to join them in celebrating this ever to be remembered " Independence Day."

ORDER OF THE DAY.

Gun at Midnight,
Ringing of Bells and 13 Guns at Sunrise,
National Salute at Sunset.

The Procession will form at half past 10 o'clock A. M., under the directions of the Marshal of the Day and his Aids, in front of R. E. Ash's Hotel, in the following order :

Artillery,
Band,
President of the Day, and Revolutionary Soldiers,
Committee of Arrangements,
ORATOR AND READER,
Clergy and Physicians,
Soldiers of the War of 1812,
Soldiers of the War with Mexico,
Town and County Officers,
Citizens in general,
Youths.

Thirty-three juvenile ladies will represent the States, and form in procession with the adult ladies, to whom a suitable place in the Procession will be assigned.

The Procession will then march to the Pine Grove, where an Oration will be delivered.

Address to the Throne of Grace, by Rev. James Quinlin.
Reading Declaration of Independence, by Henry H. Rosa.
Discharge of Cannon.
Music.
ORATION—By Hon. Geo. S. Batcheller, of Saratoga co.
Discharge of Cannon.
Music.
Vocal Music.
Benediction, by Rev. Orren Gregg.

The Procession will then form as before, and march to R. E. Ash's Hotel, where dinner will be in readiness.

Toasts will be delivered.

GRAND AND SPLENDID DISPLAY OF

FIRE-WORKS,

Will be exhibited at half past 8,

IN THE EVENING, NORTH OF THE PRESBYTERIAN CHUCH.

NORTHVILLE, JUNE 27, 1859.

G. LEFEVRE, MARSHAL.

S. Heron, Printer, Northville.

mer, Edwin Drake would drill the first U.S. oil well in Titusville, Pa., and a new U.S. flag would be hoisted up American flagpoles.

Northville itself was a growing village. Located in the Fulton County town of Northampton, it boasted three churches, four mitten factories and about 450 residents (circa 1860), according to J.H. French's Historical and Statistical Gazetteer of New York State, published in 1861. Fulton County, named after steamship inventor Robert Fulton, was the center of the buckskin leather glove industry in the United States.

On June 27, 1859, Northville's guest speaker was the Hon. George Sherman Batcheller. At 21 years of age and a recent graduate of Harvard Law School, Batcheller was practicing law in Saratoga Springs and was a freshman member of the New York State Assembly. He grew up about 5 miles away from Northville in the Saratoga County town of Edinburg.

The Assemblyman's grandfather, Ambrose Batcheller, made a fortune from lumber in the Sacandaga River Valley and founded a hamlet called Batchellerville, which is currently located on County Route 7 on the southern shore of the Great Sacandaga Lake (gates on the river's Conklingville dam were closed in 1930, creating the lake). Northville, on the northern shore of the lake, and Batchellerville are located in the southeastern corner of the Adirondack Park.

George Sherman Batcheller was born on July 25, 1837 in the town of Edinburg. A lawyer by trade, he was a New York State Assemblyman in 1859, 1873-74, 1886 and 1888-89, according to the Political Graveyard (Web site). He was a lieutenant colonel in the New York 115th Volunteer Infantry during the Civil War, a member of the Military Order of the Loyal Legion in the United States, the U.S. consul general to Portugal in 1890-92 and the American representative on the International Tribunal in Egypt. He died on July 3, 1908.

Batcheller's former Victorian home, built in 1873 in Saratoga Springs, is now operated as the Batcheller Mansion Inn.

It was fitting that George Sherman Batcheller be the guest speaker at Northville's 1859 Independence Day celebration; he was a descendant of Roger Sherman, who signed the Declaration of Independence 83 years earlier. Sherman had been a member of the Continental Congress (1774-81), the Connecticut Legislature, the U.S. House of Representatives and the U.S. Senate.

The June 27 celebration began with the shooting of a gun at midnight. At sunrise, bells began ringing around town, and a 13-gun salute was held. At 10:30 a.m., the Fourth of July marshal, G. Lefevre, led a procession in front of Ash's Hotel in the following order: artillery, band, president of the day, Revolutionary War soldiers, Committee of Arrangements, Assemblyman Batcheller, Henry Rosa, clergy and physicians, soldiers of the War of 1812, soldiers of the War with Mexico, town and county officers, citizens and youths. This group was followed by the 33 young ladies and their adult chaperones.

The procession ended at the village's Pine Grove, where Batcheller gave his speech, Rosa read the Declaration of Independence, music was played, a cannon was fired and clergymen addressed the Throne of Grace and gave the Benediction. They returned to Ash's Hotel for dinner and watched a fireworks display at 8:30 p.m. north of the First United Presbyterian Church, which still stands today on Reed Street. It was built in 1857.

Note the time of the fireworks: "half past 8." This was before Daylight Savings Time, even before the U.S. officially adopted standard time in 1918 (U.S. and Canadian railroads created standard time zones in 1883).

The Northville poster is currently in storage in the Adirondack Museum's library.

Chapter 20

Grace Brown's hair

In July 1906, the tiny Adirondack hamlet of Big Moose made national headlines. A murder will sometimes do that.

Over the past 100 years, North Country residents have turned the Chester Gillette-Grace Brown murder trial into folklore. The "Ballad of Big Moose Lake," as recalled by folk singer Dan Berggren and his mother, Dorothy Wilson Berggren, on the album, "Rooted in the Mountains," tells the story.

"They started out on their vacation, on the beautiful Big Moose Lake. Did she think as she plucked those white lilies, that her young and sweet life he would take ..."

The Adirondack Museum has several volumes of "Grace Brown's Love Letters" to Gillette, reprinted by the Citizen Publishing Company, of Herkimer. They were read to Gillette's jury, as evidence, in the Herkimer Court House on Nov. 20, 1906. Strangely enough, the Museum also has a strand of Brown's hair in its library collection.

Chester Gillette, a 23-year-old central New York man, was convicted of killing 20-year-old Grace Brown, a young, impressionable farm girl who was carrying his baby. Subsequently, the state of New York put Gillette to death at its Auburn facility after a lengthy and sensational trial.

The crime scene was the Glenmore Hotel on Big Moose Lake in Herkimer County. More accurately, the crime scene was the lake itself. Accompanying Brown's hair is a small envelope with the words "Hair of Grace Brown, Drowned, Big Moose, July 11, 06" on the front. Roy Higby found the hair after the murder and kept it for posterity. For many decades after the trial, the media lifted Higby to celebrity status, interviewing him relentlessly for anniversary editions of the story. After all, at 13 years of age, he witnessed the couple's Big Moose arrival.

The couple spent a night in Utica and another in Tupper Lake, eating a meal at Myer Newman's "Alta Cliff" Cottage in Tupper Lake. Then Gillette and Brown took the train to Big Moose. Upon arrival on July 11, 1906, a buckboard took them from the Big Moose railroad station to the Glenmore.

Higby's uncle, Dwight Sperry, owned the Big Moose Transportation Company and the Glenmore Hotel at the west end of Big Moose Lake. The buckboards brought passengers to the hotel pier,

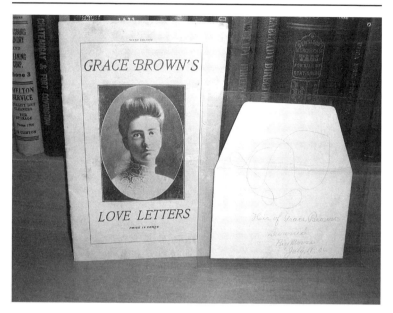

A copy of "Grace Brown's Love Letters" and a strand of Brown's hair

(Photo courtesy of the Adirondack Museum)

where they were transferred to the steamer—the 40-foot Zilpha. Higby was a purser, collecting fares and helping out with baggage and freight.

"On July 11th 1906, a young man and an attractive young lady came to the Glenmore on the buckboard arriving about noon and registered as Carl Graham and wife of Albany," Higby wrote in his account of the day. He wrote to the Museum staff, "I am asked by so many persons annually to tell this story that I feel the best solution is to put my memory of this famous case into print."

The couple had lunch at the hotel and soon rented a St. Lawrence skiff for a row around the lake.

"Graham, as he was then known to us, took with him his suitcase, tennis racket, top coat, and umbrella, while his wife left her bag and jacket and purse in her bedroom at the Glenmore," Higby wrote.

"While the boatman noticed this and thought it unusual, he did not comment at the time. This was the last seen of them together."

The couple failed to show up for dinner and the next day's breakfast. At about 11 a.m. on July 12, a search party found the capsized boat off the south shore of the lake. The Zilpha towed several guideboats and anchored near the scene, and the crew used gang fish hooks and sections of stove pipe to look for the drowned bodies on the bottom of the lake. When they found Brown's body, the Zilpha's engineer snagged her dress with a pike pole, and several men pulled her out of the water. During the process, several strands of her hair were lodged in the gunwale of the skiff. Higby wrapped the hair in tissue paper as a souvenir.

"Somewhere in my safe I have a lock of Grace Brown's hair that I took from the gunwale of the boat and my mother preserved through the years," Higby wrote.

Gillette was arrested at the Arrowhead Hotel at Fourth Lake the next day and brought to the Glenmore, where he was identified as "Carl Graham." A trial that captured the nation's attention followed through the fall months.

Gillette was convicted of Brown's murder on Dec. 6, 1906 and killed in the electric chair on March 30, 1908. At the execution, he admitted to dumping Brown's body in Big Moose Lake after beating her with a tennis racket.

When Higby died at the age of 97, one of the strands of Brown's hair was donated to the Adirondack Museum. It is stashed away with the envelope, in a plastic bag, in a folder with pink-covered copies of "Grace Brown's Love Letters" in a humidity- and temperature-controlled room in the Museum's library.

Brown's love letters began in April 1906 and ended in July. Her tone was cheerful at first. Then she moved home after learning she was pregnant. When Gillette ignored her and she heard about his flings with other women, Brown's words became gloomy. Her last letter to Gillette, dated July 6, 1906, is an eerie prophecy of her fate in the Adirondacks.

"My Dear Chester, I am curled up by the kitchen fire and you would shout if you could see me ... I will never be happy again, dear. I wish I could die. You never know what you have made me suffer, dear. I miss you and I want to see you but I wish I could die ..."

The murder inspired Theodore Dreiser's 1925 novel, "An American Tragedy," and the Academy Award-winning 1951 movie, "A Place in the Sun," starring Montgomery Clift and Elizabeth Taylor. In 1986, Craig Brandon published a non-fiction account of the murder and trial, "Murder in the Adirondacks: An American Tragedy Revisited."

Chapter 21

Original Westport chair

Buyer beware. Many of the Adirondack Westport chairs on the market today look nothing like the original.

Since the first "Adirondack" chair was designed more than 100 years ago, it has been transformed into the variety of chairs we see today. Some are made of South American mahogany, recycled old-growth western red cedar, yellow cedar, California sugar pine or white pine. Some are widened and made into love seats. Some come with matching ottomans. Many found in American and Canadian back yards are made of plastic, and most Adirondack chairs sold today have multiple slats for the backrest.

Aha! The Westport chair, as the first Adirondack-style chairs were called, only had one wide board for its backrest. If you have any doubts, sit in one yourself; the Adirondack Museum has a number of brown replicas scattered around its Blue Mountain Lake campus. It also has an original Westport chair (artifact No. 62.31) made by Harry C. Bunnell in the Essex County village of Westport.

Yet even Bunnell, who was granted a patent for his Westport chair design in 1905, wasn't the real Adirondack chair inventor. That distinction goes to Thomas Lee.

Around 1900, Lee modestly designed a wooden chair for his Westport property. He wasn't trying to invent a product that would make him millions. He merely wanted a comfortable chair for private use.

Bunnell, his friend, needed cash, so Lee suggested that he copy the chair's design and sell the copies. Bunnell knew a good thing when he saw it and jumped at the opportunity. He borrowed the chair. Boy, did he borrow the chair! Bunnell filed a patent for the design, and then he manufactured and sold them for more than 20 years.

In his patent, filed with the U.S. Patent Office, Bunnell wrote, "The object of this invention is a chair of the bungalow type adapted for use on porches, lawns, at camps, and also adapted to be converted into an invalid's chair."

Following Bunnell's success, another model, the Adirondack chair, was created. Now the style is famous worldwide.

In its summer/autumn 1912 "Adirondack Outfittings" catalog, W.C. Leonard & Co. in Saranac Lake sold what it called "Bunnell's Adirondack Bungalow Chair" for $10.

An original Westport chair, artifact No. 62.31, built by Harry C. Bunnell
(Photo courtesy of the Adirondack Museum)

"The simple, graceful lines, handsome exclusive design, rich appearance and luxurious, restful comfort, combined in this chair, appeal strongly to lovers of things that are oddly beautiful—besides being extremely comfortable."

Every inch of the chair was handmade from selected Adirondack woods, according to Leonard's catalog.

"Try a couple of these chairs on your porch or in your library. Your family and your guests will prefer them to any other chair, outdoors or indoors, solely because they are so very, very restful."

The featured Westport chair (artifact No. 62.31) was purchased in 1914. It was donated to the Adirondack Museum in 1962 by a Keene Valley woman. Its dimensions are: 37.25 inches (height) by 39.5 inches (width) and 35.5 inches (depth). The chair is made from planks instead of narrow boards, and the maker's mark is stamped on the back of the chair: "U.S. Pat. July 18, 1905/Mfd. By H.C. Bunnell/Westport, N.Y."

The current surface of the Museum's Westport chair is a modern brown paint, which was cleaned in 1964. The original color was a reddish brown, today known in the Adirondacks as Johnsburg Red. Bunnell did not paint his chairs; he finished the wood with brown stain and coated them with wax for outdoor use.

The wood, hemlock, intrigued those who analyzed the chair in the 1980s. Staffers at the State University of New York College of Environmental Science and Forestry conducted a wood analysis in 1983, and an expert said that hemlock trees 20 inches in diameter or larger are not usually cut for lumber. Smaller ones are cut, but not much lumber can be used from them. The use of hemlock in the Westport chair was deemed "somewhat unusual."

This particular chair is currently in storage; however, it had been temporarily displayed at the Adirondack Museum's Adirondack Cottage.

In 1963, the chair caught the eye of antique gurus Ralph and Terry Kovel, who are famous for their collectible guides and currently have a television show called "Flea Market Finds" on Home and Garden Television (HGTV). The Kovels asked for and received permission to use a photograph of the Westport chair in an antique book. In a Jan. 29, 1964 letter to "Ralph and Terry Kovel, Know Your Antiques, Shaker Heights, Ohio," an Adirondack Museum official sent them three black-and-white photos of the chair with the stipulation that proper credit should be given to the Blue Mountain Lake facility.

Chapter 22

Devil Bug fishing lures

It's a colorful bug with a large stinger on the rump and an eye-hole for a mouth. Found in lakes and rivers, garages, closets and boats, it's the genuine Adirondack Devil Bug.

Orley C. Tuttle (1876-1943), inventor and original manufacturer of Tuttle Devil Bugs in Old Forge after World War I, guaranteed that his product "offers sportsmen lures that are real fish-getters and made from the best of materials."

All lures added to the Devil Bug line were first scrutinized and tested in Adirondack waterways. Tuttle, himself, "personally experimented in various waters and perfected them until proven fish-getters." The Adirondack Museum has a collection of Tuttle Devil Bugs of all shapes and sizes. One is the Winged Bass Devil Bug (artifact No. 74.281) and another is the Trout Devil Bug (77.69.1).

The Devil Bug family includes the Famous Devil Bug Mouse with long tail, Trout Mouse, Muskie Mouse, Original Bass Devil Bug, Trout Devil Bug, Fly Rod Special Devil Bug, Midget Devil Bug (a "Dry Fly"), Wet Fly Devil Bug, "Top-Knot" Devil Bug, Tuttle's Whirlo Minnow, Tuttle's New Style Bucktail, Tuttle's Trolling Spoons, and Tuttle's Trolling Spoon with Bucktail.

Tuttle owned a resort on the south shore of Fourth Lake and was an avid fisherman. Inspired by a beetle-eating bass in 1919, the Devil Bug grew out of Tuttle's imagination and his determination to mimic nature so he could catch more fish. The first Devil Bug, covered in deer hair and designed to look like a beetle, worked so well that he began manufacturing the lures. His wife, Lottie (1878-1936), painted the Devil Bugs and made remarkable illustrations for the brochures and poster advertisements.

Tuttle's Devil Bugs soon became staples in Adirondack tackle boxes. In 1922, they sold more than 50,000 Devil Bugs, according to a Spring 1975 article in Adirondack Life magazine. Tuttle's daughter and son-in-law, Edith and Clarence Morcy, took over the business in 1935. After Mr. Morcy's death, the business was sold to Old Forge art teacher Al Stripp in July 1974.

The Museum's Winged Bass Devil Bug (74.281), donated by Stripp on Oct. 4, 1974, was probably made by the new manufacturers, either Stripp or Eddie Tuttle Morris. It is still in the original box.

An old Tuttle's Devil Bugs catalog (no date) explains the variety of the

Winged Bass Devil Bug (artifact No. 74.281), left, and Trout Devil Bug (77.69.1) fishing lures made by the O.C. Tuttle Devil Bug Co., Old Forge

(Photo courtesy of the Adirondack Museum)

lures and gives directions on how they should be used.

"TUTTLE DEVIL BUGS float, crunch and taste like real bugs and millers," the catalog states. "Fish hold and swallow them as the deer's hair of which they are made retains a faint saline taste. Because of the action of water upon deer's hair and the realistic formation of Devil Bugs, they look ALIVE!"

The Winged Bass Devil Bug (size 1/0) is made out of dyed deer hair and has a red body with white stripe down the back and black and yellow eyes. It also came in the following colors: gray and red, all gray, all white, all brown, and black and yellow. It is 1.75 inches long. The Devil Bugs used for bass fishing included the Devil Bug Mouse, Original Bass Devil Bug and Winged Bass Bugs. They were used as surface lures during the day and night.

"When a Devil Bug Mouse or a Bass Bug is cast to the edge of a lily pad, stump, rock or favorite hiding place, Mr. Bass gets busy and the battle is on," the catalog states. "Many times, especially at night, when a bass 'smacks' the bug he doesn't take it in his mouth far enough at the sound of the 'smack' and often times (if the fisherman strikes at that time) he will loose [sic] the bass. When they are doing this, count three slowly after the 'smack' and then strike hard. You will have Mr. Bass and find he has the bug well into his mouth."

The Museum's Trout Devil Bug (77.69.1) never made it to a tackle box; it was simply purchased at Old Forge Hardware on April 25, 1977. It is 0.75 inches long and has red and white deer hair. It was also available in dark gray, black and white, light gray, brown and green, and gray and red.

Trout Devil Bugs were designed to closely resemble moths and millers. As they are cast onto the water, the lures "spread their wings" as if they are alive.

"They can be fished, one, two or three on a leader," the catalog states. "The most perfect action is obtained by using a 6-foot leader with droppers 2 feet apart, using three bugs–a size 10 top fly to flutter on the water and size 8 for tail fly, the center fly being optional. Cast lightly upon the water, allow to remain still for a second, then retrieve slowly, imitating by a slight trembling motion of the hand, the fluttering of a miller. Give the trout more time than is used with ordinary flies."

These particular Tuttle Devil Bugs are currently in storage; however, visitors can find Tuttle lures in the Museum's exhibit, "Woods and Waters: Outdoor Recreation in the Adirondacks."

Chapter 23

Mountaineering boots

Footwear is one of the most essential items on a rock climber's equipment list, and picking the right pair of boots is like picking the right set of tires for a backcountry-bound truck. Make sure they have adequate traction and they're tough and durable enough to tear through dirt, mud, ice and snow.

Prior to World War II, serious mountain climbing boots resembled metal-studded snow tires rather than high-performance sport radials. Long before Vibram and Fusion 3 rubber soles were invented, Adirondack climbers such as Arthur "Bob" Notman Jr. used two kinds of footwear: heavy metal-studded boots and lighter rope-soled shoes. The Adirondack Museum has an assortment of Notman's climbing gear in its collection, including his metal-soled boots, artifacts No. 78.11.31 a/b (currently in storage).

In the 1930s, Notman climbed Adirondack precipices with these brown, leather boots, size 11.5. Handmade by a boot maker in the Alps, they have loops at the back of the boots so Notman could pull them on his feet. The top of each boot is rimmed with heavy felt and leather.

Notman, who died early in World War II, was active in promoting rock climbing and winter mountaineering in the Adirondacks during the Great Depression. He made many "first ascents" in the High Peaks region with people such as legendary climber and German expatriate Fritz Weissner and former American Alpine Club President John Case. When Adirondack Museum officials were in the process of planning and installing the "Woods and Waters: Outdoor Recreation in the Adirondacks" exhibit, they were looking for artifacts that fit the theme: fishing tackle, hunting firearms, and rock climbing and winter mountaineering gear.

If there's one hamlet in the Adirondack Park that best represents the extreme sports of rock climbing and winter mountaineering, it's Keene Valley in Essex County. Just stop by the Cliffhanger Café. See the mountaineering volumes in the Keene Valley Library. Better yet, order a piece of pie at the Noon Mark Diner and listen; you're bound to hear a story or two about multiple-pitch climbs on the Chapel Pond Slab.

With the help of James Goodwin, of the Keene Valley-based Adirondack Trail Improvement Society, the Adirondack Museum

Adirondack rock climbing boots, artifacts No. 78.11.31 a/b, worn by Arthur "Bob" Notman Jr. in the 1930s

(Photo courtesy of the Adirondack Museum)

acquired Notman's climbing equipment. Notman's brother made the donation in 1978, and Goodwin provided the Museum with biographical information about the mountaineer.

The equipment includes hemp ropes, pitons imported from Austria and Switzerland, and imported ice axes and crampons, all of which were used in Adirondack winter ascents of the Mount Colden Trap Dyke and in the cirque of Giant Mountain.

The Notman family's association with the Adirondacks began with Bob's grandfather, George Notman, who first visited the Adirondacks in 1874. He was 21 years old at the time and spent six summer weeks in Keene Valley. He liked the town so much, he bought property there. In 1885, he built a camp called Eaglestowe.

Born in 1915, Bob Notman spent the summers of his childhood and college years with his family in Keene Valley. He enjoyed climbing mountains in the High Peaks region, and when he was a teenager, he met fellow summer resident John Case. Before and after World War I, Case had traveled through the European Alps to make ascents, and he is credited with founding technical rock climbing in the Adirondacks in 1916.

Case's influence on Notman was profound. The teenager learned about rock climbing by making many Adirondack first ascents with Case during the 1930s. Inspired by the master, Notman began leading climbs and organizing his own trips. He was president of the Harvard Mountaineering Club in 1937 and organized a climbing expedition to the Canadian Rockies and Selkirk Mountains of British Columbia.

In 1938, Notman invited Weissner to make new climbs in the Adirondacks and coach rock climbers. Weissner, who moved to the U.S. from Germany in the late 1930s, took him up on the offer. Together with Becket Howarth, of the Appalachian Mountain Club, they climbed several of the major cliff faces in the Adirondack Mountains, including the center chimney section of Wallface above Indian Pass.

Further inspired, summer rock climbing led to winter ice climbing. In December 1938, Notman and a friend made what may have been the first winter ascent of a rock bluff, or knob, on the Chapel Pond Slab, southwest of Chapel Pond. After Notman died in World War II, his climbing friends named the bluff in his memory. It is simply called "Bob's Knob."

"Bob Notman's leadership in Adirondack mountaineering during the 1930s set the stage for what was to come in post-war years," Goodwin wrote to the Adirondack Museum. "(His) enthusiasm and initiative played a major part in making Adirondack mountaineering what it has become today."

Notman had pioneered a number of routes on the Chapel Pond Slab, which is now one of the most popular Adirondack climbing areas. Bob's Knob Standard (5.3) is a 700-foot climb, even though it is mainly used today as a descent, according to Don Mellor's guidebook, "Climbing in the Adirondacks," published by the Adirondack Mountain Club. On the rock climbing scale—5.0 being the easiest and 5.14 the most difficult—Bob's Knob includes routes called Eagle Crack (5.7), Hamburger Helper (5.8) and Dog's Breakfast (5.11).

Prior to World War II, most alpine climbers used nailed boots and carried rope-soled shoes in their packs (for difficult pitches). According to Goodwin, rope was better than sneaker rubber on wet rock, and although many Adirondack climbers used sneakers, Notman and his friends preferred the nailed boot/rope-soled shoe combination. The production of Vibram-soled boots in northern Italy in the 1940s made nailed boots obsolete.

Chapter 24

Dr. Arpad Gerster's sketches, silk tent

Silk is used for bedding, hosiery, underwear and robes. Tuscan farmers use silk parachutes to harvest olives. It seems this natural fabric, sought after for its smoothness and "breathing" qualities, was also perfect for Adirondack fishing trips in the 19th century.

Outdoorsmen prefer lighter gear when they can get it, and in the pre-synthetic fabric days, silk was a good option for those who could afford it. Dr. Arpad Geyza Gerster, a noted New York City surgeon, used a silk tent when fishing and camping in the Adirondack Mountains in the late 1800s and early 1900s.

Gerster (1848-1923) had owned camps on Raquette and Long lakes in Hamilton County, and the lightness of his tent allowed him to travel through the backcountry with ease, doing what he liked best—fishing and sketching. The tent, artifact No. 58.333 in the Adirondack Museum's collection, dates to about 1890 and includes an attached fly, a cotton cheesecloth-like bug screen for the front. It was made in A-frame style and has cotton canvas tape to reinforce the edges. It is 66.5 inches wide, 50 inches high and 88 inches long, and tree branches were used for tent poles.

On his mountain trips, Gerster liked to sketch the people and places he encountered, and he soon became a proficient artist. He translated these drawings into prints using etched metal plates. Etching is a process where prints are created by an image being "etched" below the surface of a material (copper, zinc or iron plates). Prints of the image are then produced by filling the detail of the etching with ink and pressing it against paper.

In 1998, Gerster was featured in the book "Adirondack Prints and Printmakers: The Call of the Wild," edited by Adirondack Museum Chief Curator and Director of Operations Caroline Welsh. She also wrote Chapter 8, a paper titled "A Passion for Fishing and Tramping: The Adirondacks Etched by Arpad G. Gerster, M.D."

The Museum owns a number of items that once belonged to Gerster, including the sketch book and three sketches featured in this week's column. They were donated by a Long Lake resident in 1958 and are currently in storage. The 4-by-6-inch black sketch book still has the original price sticker inside—30 cents.

Gerster included the silk tent in two of this week's drawings, one on Carry Point (1892) and the other at the "Sucker Brook Camp"

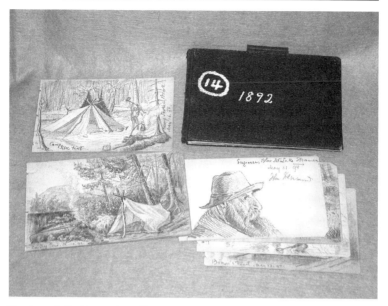

Dr. Arpad G. Gerster's Adirondack sketches from the 1890s

(Photo courtesy of the Adirondack Museum)

(1894). The third sketch (1894) is of John Hammond, former engineer on the Blue Mountain Lake steamer.

Other sketches in the Museum's collection include the family pet, Little Forked Stream, rowing on Seventh Lake, a scene near the outlet of Raquette Lake, guide Alvah Dunning sleeping between roots of a large tree, and Constable Point on Raquette Lake.

"Etching is a domestic occupation which can be followed in town during odds hours; it can be interrupted at pleasure without inconvenience, and offers most refreshing diversion from the exhausting tension of busy professional life. Nothing in the world can make a man forget himself and his cares more quickly than the etcher's needle," Gerster wrote in his 1917 autobiography, "Recollections of a New York City Surgeon."

"Adirondack Prints and Printmakers" includes a dozen of Gerster's prints, such as "My Camp at Carry Point," etched in September 1892. It is almost identical to the original pencil drawing I found in one of Gerster's sketchbooks for this week's column.

The print and the sketch, however, are flipped horizontally, which makes sense. The plate was copied from the sketch, so any print made from the plate would naturally be backwards. Otherwise, they both have the same placement of the tent, campfire, ax in a log, and canoe, and the trees and the mountain in the background are the same. Gerster did make two significant changes to the original sketch when he needled the "My Camp at Carry Point" etching; he added a man, carrying a pail next to the canoe, and an oar, leaning against a tree behind the tent.

In 1916, Gerster described this etching and why the destination of Carry Pond, near Forked Lake, was so special to him.

"I used to make this trip without a guide, camping on the way, doing all the work, to reduce flesh and to strengthen the heart muscle. It was a delightful experience. A 12-foot cedar canoe built ad hoc, weighing 34 lbs., a silk tent, 5 lbs., a light axe, blankets, an aluminum cooking kit, one or two days' provisions, a small rifle with ball and shot cartridges, a map, sketchbook and tobacco, made an outfit I could easily handle ... Truly a paradisiacal existence, and the sweetest balm for the jaded nerves of a metropolitan surgeon."

Gerster was born on Dec. 22, 1848 in Kassa, Hungary, and he earned a degree in medicine in 1872 at the University of Vienna. He moved to the United States in 1874, settling in New York City. He practiced medicine and taught at a variety of places from 1878 to 1914, including Mount Sinai, New York Polyclinic and the College of Physicians and Surgeons at Columbia University. In 1888, he published a groundbreaking textbook, "Rules of Aseptic and Antiseptic Surgery."

Gerster began summering in the Adirondacks in 1883 when he briefly visited the Hemlocks hotel at Raquette Lake. He returned to Raquette Lake the following year with his family and stayed in a cabin near Ed Bennett's hotel. Later in the season, they moved to a Raquette Lake camp (Oteetiwi) on Big Island, where they summered until selling Oteetiwi in 1905. They moved their summer headquarters in 1906 to a 90-acre tract of land on the western shore of Long Lake. That was the last summer Gerster spent in the Adirondacks.

The silk tent and the sketches featured this week are currently in storage at the Adirondack Museum, but visitors can see Gerster's former outhouse any day of the week. Located on the Museum campus next to the Blue Mountain House hotel, the "Rustic Privy" (No. 4 on the Museum's site map) came from Gerster's Camp Kwenogamak on Long Lake.

Chapter 25

Log-splitting explosive wedge

Splitting logs for the wood pile? Get yourself an explosive wedge, gun powder, fuses and a light. That's what some loggers did half a century ago in the Northeast.

The Adirondack Museum owns a rounded explosive wedge (artifact No. 86.48) made of heavy iron. It is 14.75 inches long and 2.75 inches in diameter and was used as a log splitter. Typically the iron cylinder includes a cavity at the small end, a fuse hole on one side and a small chain with red fabric flag attached to the other side. The flag in this case is missing. The wedge is currently in storage with other logging artifacts.

Mr. and Mrs. John Dunham, of Sparks, Md., donated the wedge to the Museum in 1986. It had been used in Adirondack logging camps.

Information about this particular wedge was not found in the Museum's records; however, the Lumber Camp News published a report on explosive wedges in its June 1951 issue. Fred Simmons, a former logging specialist for the Northeastern Forest Experiment Station in the U.S. Department of Agriculture's Forest Service, wrote the article, which was first published in the "Northeastern Loggers' Handbook," January 1951.

The rounded explosive wedge had apparently evolved from a crude form of log splitting.

"For several years, timber operators have been using black powder instead of wedges for splitting," Simmons wrote.

Loggers bored holes 0.75 to 1 inch in diameter in the top side of the logs. Then black powder or slow-burning dynamite was tamped into each hole. A fuse or blasting cap was inserted, "and the whole thing is tamped tight with dry leaves, wadded paper, or some similar substance."

Simmons reported that an electric firing machine and blasting caps were preferred to fuses for this work, especially if they were set off in a series, because they were more reliable and the charges could be more easily set off simultaneously.

Simmons explained that the explosive wedge, a "new development" at the time, was becoming more popular with timber harvesters. Instead of simply tamping black powder or dynamite into a hole in a log, two kinds of iron explosive wedges could be used: the flat type and the round type.

Explosive wedge, artifact No. 86.48, used for splitting trees in Adirondack logging camps

(Photo courtesy of the Adirondack Museum)

The flat type, resembling a small shovel, could be driven into either side or end of the log. The round type, which looked like a large bullet, could only be driven into the end of the "stick." The round type was generally used for shorter logs, yet it had been used for logs up to 10 feet in length.

Loggers put black powder inside the iron cylinder and placed a fuse in the side hole. The splitter was then wedged into a notch at the top of a felled tree. After the fuse was set, Simmons wrote, "A block of wood is placed against the exposed end of the wedge to keep it from kicking out too far, and the charge is set off."

The explosion would split the tree, and the red flag was used to help locate the splitter afterward.

The original rounded wedge, the "Webber Splitting Gun," was developed on the West Coast and was primarily used in splitting softwood for fuel.

"Its driving edge is too wide-angled, and its head is too soft for continued use with hardwoods. Special wedges of the same type, designed primarily for hardwoods, have been placed on the market in the Northeast," Simmons wrote.

The Forest Service made sure that timber operators knew how to safely use the explosive wedges, and the "Northeastern Loggers' Handbook" published the following safety tips:

1. No person should smoke while handling, storing, transporting, or working around powder.
2. Fuses should be kept clean and dry, and precautions should be taken against their being kinked or abraded. No fuse that is wet, oil-soaked, kinked, or damaged in any way should be used.
3. Metal tools should not be used around powder, especially in opening powder boxes.
4. Frozen powder should be thawed only in small quantities by using preheated water in a water-jacketed vessel. It should never be thawed by means of an open fire, steam, hot water contact, or an electrical heating device.
5. Wooden tools should be used in tamping powder into place.
6. When the shot is fired, timely warning should be given, and it should be heeded by everyone exposed to danger. If the shot does not go off, no one should go near it for at least half an hour.

Chapter 26

Noah John Rondeau statue

A life-sized statue of Adirondack hermit Noah John Rondeau (1883-1967) stands frozen in time, wielding an ax, at his Cold River City encampment. No mosquitoes or conservation officers can pester him now inside this air-conditioned Adirondack Museum exhibit—population one wooden replica of the 5-foot, 2-inch monster of a legend.

The statue, artifact No. 78.51 in the Museum's collection, actually stands more than 6.5 feet tall since the ax is lifted above Rondeau's head, ready to swing down and chop a notch in a hardwood log. "His swing has the strength and precision born of long experience in the woods," stated the Adirondack Museum news release dated May 24, 1978.

That's when the world learned that part of Rondeau's former hermitage—the Hall of Records and Beauty Parlor wigwam—would be moved from the Museum's grounds into the new "Woods and Waters" exhibit. A newly donated statue of Rondeau was to be included.

The statue, carved out of a block of white pine that was laminated from smaller pieces, was the creation of sculptor Robert Longhurst. Born in Schenectady and a 1969 graduate of Adirondack Community College in Glens Falls, Longhurst earned a bachelor's degree in architecture from Ohio's Kent State University in 1975.

Asked why he wanted to carve a statue of Rondeau, Longhurst said at the time, "It's my salute to the Adirondacks."

Longhurst worked six days a week for three months in his Cincinnati studio to complete the sculpture. It was shipped from there to the Blue Mountain Lake facility in May 1978.

At first, the Museum's director at the time, Craig Gilborn, was skeptical of Longhurst's offer to make a wooden statue of Rondeau. It was nothing personal, as he explained in a May 17, 1978 thank-you letter to the sculptor. In past experiences, Gilborn had dealt with artists whose "enthusiasm and conviction" exceeded their talent. This time, though, the director was pleasantly surprised with the finished product.

"Your figure is very fine indeed ... You have captured Rondeau's prickly character; the deep folds and ridges in the clothing masterfully convey this and lends movement to the sculpture," Gilborn wrote.

Praise cascaded from the visiting public as well. It didn't take long for the Rondeau statue to become a popular feature in the exhibit.

The wooden statue of hermit Noah John Rondeau, artifact No. 78.51, was placed among his original belongings at the Adirondack Museum's "Woods and Waters" exhibit in 1978.

(Photo courtesy of the Adirondack Museum)

Rondeau grew up in the Au Sable Forks area. His first trip to the Cold River country was in 1902, according to Maitland De Sormo's book, "Noah John Rondeau: Adirondack Hermit." Rondeau was hunting and searching for trapping grounds. He lived in Lake Placid until 1913 or 1914, working as a barber and doing other odd jobs and then moved to Coreys, east of Tupper Lake.

"There he found a form of work that was far more appealing to his nature—guiding and trapping," De Sormo wrote.

Rondeau set trap lines throughout the Cold River region and began wintering there in 1929. Moving his residence a few times in the backcountry, he finally settled on what we know today as Rondeau's Hermitage, on a high bluff overlooking Cold River. At the time, the land was owned by the Santa Clara Lumber Company. The Northville-Placid Trail, built in 1922, passes through the site.

Rondeau would make trips to Coreys and Saranac Lake for supplies. He also had many visitors, hikers mainly from the Adirondack Mountain Club or aspiring Adirondack 46'ers, who brought him food. His longest continuous stay at Cold River was 381 days (May 1, 1943 - May 16, 1944)

The hermit called Cold River his home until after the "Big Blow" hurricane knocked down thousands of trees in the fall of 1950. The Conservation Department then closed the Cold River region to the public for several years.

Even before 1950, Rondeau took pleasure in touring outdoor recreation shows in the Northeast and became a celebrity in New York City. He traveled with a replica of his Cold River City—the Town Hall, wigwams and Hall of Records. Rondeau's appointments increased after leaving the woods, and he even played the part of Santa Claus for several years at the Santa's Workshop theme park in the town of Wilmington.

In the spring of 1957, the Hall of Records and Beauty Parlor wigwam were dismantled and moved to the Adirondack Museum, where they were eventually put on display outside. Rondeau sold dozens of his belongings to the Museum in 1958.

Rondeau died in the Lake Placid hospital on Aug. 24, 1967 and was buried in the North Elba Cemetery. A rock with a plaque marks his grave. Lake Placid, however, was not the hermit's choice for his final resting place. Rondeau spent years at the Hermitage planting flowers and grooming his own burial plot on the high bluff overlooking Cold River. His spirit is still there, on what is now state land—part of the High Peaks Wilderness Area.

As for Longhurst, the sculptor moved to Crown Point in 1979 and now owns a studio at Potterbrook Farm in Chestertown. Some of his work can be seen on his Web site, www.robertlonghurst.com.

Chapter 27

Precision power chain saw

The Adirondack Mountains attract people who value their independence. Yet even economic do-it-yourselfers have to rely on something, whether it's the volume of tourists each summer, efficient snow removal each winter or a fresh stand of trees ready to be harvested.

Gilbert Patton (1917-1994) was such a man. A logger by trade, he relished his freedom, yet he relied on good horses, a good hardware store and a good chain saw to put food on the table.

The Adirondack Museum owns one of Patton's chain saws, a Precision power chain saw made in Canada. It is artifact No. 2002.72 in the Museum's collection (currently in storage), and Patton's family donated the power tool in his memory in November 2002.

In 1945, Gilbert and Mary Patton moved to Bakers Mills, in the Warren County town of Johnsburg, from the Owego area, where they had a farm. They also had three children: Theodore, Robert and Kathryn.

Mary Patton suffered from asthma, and her doctor recommended that she get away from farm country. As a part-time truck driver, Gilbert Patton had learned about Bakers Mills while making deliveries along Route 8 in the southern Adirondacks. That's where the Pattons would settle, in a small hamlet with a grocery store and a hardware store. Their home was near the firehouse, and they kept horses for logging in a neighbor's barn.

Gilbert Patton chose logging as a new career because he wanted to continue to be self-employed. The family even transplanted some of their independent farm life at the Bakers Mills homestead; they had a garden and chickens and raised their own pork.

Gilbert Patton worked as a "cutter" for himself and for a few logging jobbers, and he sold logs to the Murphy sawmill in Chestertown. Sometimes he would get a call from a property owner who wanted his land logged. Patton then cruised the land to assess the standing timber, paid a stumpage fee to the owner and started cutting. He used horses to skid the logs and kept the animals near the job sites, traveling to work in a truck.

In the Adirondack Museum's archives, Robert Patton said his father was well-known for his colorful phrases, such as, "That's heavier than a dead preacher full of sin." Who knows, he may have said that about the Precision chain saw, which weighs between 42 and 52

Gilbert Patton's Precision power chain saw, artifact No. 2002.72

(Photo courtesy of the Adirondack Museum)

pounds, depending on the length of the guide bar. Gilbert Patton slung the chain saw over his back and took it into the woods. It was used at the log bunking ground to cut trees to length.

The chain saw—made of steel, iron and copper—is 38.5 inches long, 20.25 inches tall and 15 inches deep. The 18-inch bow saw can be removed and replaced by either of the two straight blades. With the 26-inch straight bar attachment (with a handle at one end), this one-man saw converts to a two-man unit.

Gilbert Patton possibly bought the chain saw from Charles Wade, of North Creek, around 1949. In fact, Charles S. Wade Sale & Service purchased an advertisement for this very saw in the July 1949 issue of Lumber Camp News. Plus, Robert Patton said his father bought supplies from Wade.

"CUT THEM DOWN AND SAW THEM UP with The New 1949 ONE-MAN LIGHT-WEIGHT PRECISION Power Chain Saw," the advertisement stated.

The 1949 chain saw had many improvements, including a non-flooding and non-swiveling carburetor; a high-sparking magneto ("will start easily in any weather"); a new type of air filter ("eliminates saw-dust, water or snow"); and a twist grip that combined the throttle and clutch control. At the time, all of the Precision saws used a 2-cycle, 3.5 horse power, air-cooled motor with positive clutch, and there were eight types of Precision saws that used the same motor. The interchangeable attachments were available "at (a) small extra cost."

In 1962, the Pattons moved to Wevertown, where their house burned down six months later. Then they moved into a mobile home on the same property. Mary Patton had been a postal carrier in Bakers Mills.

Chapter 28

TR's 'Night Ride' raincoat

It's been 102 years since U.S. Vice President Theodore Roosevelt made his famous "Night Ride to the Presidency" from Tahawus to the North Creek train station, and the town of Newcomb continues to celebrate the native New Yorker's connection to the High Peaks region during the annual Teddy Roosevelt Days, being held this weekend.

The Adirondack Museum owns a few artifacts from Roosevelt's 1901 trip to Newcomb, including the raincoat (artifact No. 2001.44) he was reported to have worn during the night ride.

The khaki raincoat, which is currently on display in the Museum's "Adirondacks in the Age of Horses" exhibit, is single-breasted and made of rubberized canvas. It has button cuffs with a half belt buttoned at the rear, two deep pockets (one with a change compartment) with flaps, and a buttoned vent. Many of the buttons are original, but there are some old replacements. The location of original label, long missing, is visible at neck. The coat is 51 inches tall.

There seems to be no doubt that Roosevelt wore the raincoat during his stay in the town of Newcomb. There are, however, discrepancies as to when and where he wore it.

Nevertheless, a former Adirondack Museum curator concluded that the coat's association with TR is "perfectly believable and hypothetically strong," yet it is documented in "imperfect ways."
Before explaining those imperfections, let's summarize the events leading up to the night ride on Sept. 13-14, 1901.

President William McKinley had been shot by an anarchist in Buffalo on Sept. 6, 1901, and Roosevelt arrived in Buffalo the following day. After learning that the president was safe and recovering, TR traveled to the town of Newcomb to meet his vacationing family. He arrived on Sept. 11, according to the book, "Theodore Roosevelt's Night Ride to the Presidency," written by Eloise Cronin Murphy and published by the Adirondack Museum.

The Roosevelts were staying at the Tahawus Club, and on Sept. 12, they hiked to Lake Colden and spent the night. On the morning of Sept. 13, the family returned to the Tahawus Club while the vice president, his guide Noah LaCasse, and three others climbed Mount Marcy.

"We went to the top of the mountain, walking in rain and clouds so thick we could not see ten feet ahead of us," LaCasse had told Murphy during her research.

Raincoat, artifact No. 2001.44, worn by U.S. President Theodore Roosevelt

(Photo courtesy of the Adirondack Museum)

The sky cleared for about 10 minutes while the party was on top of Mount Marcy, the highest peak in New York state at 5,344 feet. Then it clouded over again, and they headed back down the mountain to Lake Tear-of-the-Clouds, where they had lunch.

Meanwhile, McKinley's condition was deteriorating, and Roosevelt was needed in Buffalo. An urgent message was sent to the Tahawus Club's Lower Club House and written on a piece of paper. Guide Harrison Hall delivered it to Roosevelt, meeting him at Lake Tear-of-the-Clouds. TR read the note, and then he finished lunch.

Once the party returned to the Tahawus Club, the Roosevelts made preparations to leave the following day. At about 10 p.m, Roosevelt received another urgent call; this time, the message stated that it was imperative the vice president travel to Buffalo at once. That's when the night ride began.

Three men drove Roosevelt on a buckboard to North Creek, using separate teams of horses: Tahawus Club superintendent David Hunter, 10 miles to the Tahawus Post Office; Orrin Kellogg, 9 miles to the Aiden Lair hotel; and Aiden Lair owner Mike Cronin, 16 miles to the depot. It was almost dawn when they arrived in North Creek. McKinley died at 2:15 a.m., before Roosevelt arrived at Aiden Lair.

So where does the raincoat come into the scenario?

The coat was donated to the Adirondack Museum by Michael Nardacci, the great-grandson of Mike Cronin, who had displayed the artifact at his hotel for many years. The raincoat was originally owned by Roosevelt's guide, Noah LaCasse.

Unfortunately, there is no documentation about the transfer of the coat from LaCasse to Cronin. Only oral histories survive. It is said that Roosevelt wore the raincoat during his climb up Mount Marcy on Sept. 13, 1901. According to family tradition, it is also said that the coat was loaned to Roosevelt by LaCasse at the time he was sworn in as president at the North Creek train station. This could not have been true; Roosevelt was sworn in as president in Buffalo.

In Murphy's book, Kellogg recalled that Roosevelt had used one of his raincoats "to protect him from the mud splashing from the wheels." It sounds as though he pointed to the coat during the interview, as he said, "Here is my old raincoat." Of course, Roosevelt could have been wearing LaCasse's raincoat and still shield himself from the mud with Kellogg's.

Even though the exact details are lost in time, it is still accepted that Roosevelt wore the LaCasse raincoat during his famous night ride to North Creek, where he left as the 26th president of the United States.

Chapter 29

Rising District School

When the Rising District School house was built in the Herkimer County town of Ohio in 1907, Theodore Roosevelt was finishing his second term as president of the United States. When the aging one-classroom structure was moved to the Adirondack Museum 80 years later, President Ronald Reagan was serving his second term and fending off criticism about the Iran-Contra Affair.

The Rising School gives people a historical sense of time and place as they walk inside. It is an artifact itself, No. 87.78, and the classroom is decorated with other artifacts from the early 20th century: books, desks, chairs, a chalkboard and a picture of George Washington on the wall.

During the 1912-1913 school year, when Lydia Farber taught at the Rising School, a picture of President William H. Taft may have been found on the wall, or at least in one of the 255 books in the school library. When the Trustees Annual Report for the Rising School District was filed for the year ending July 31, 1913, Woodrow Wilson had just moved into the White House (Reagan was only 2 years old).

Farber earned $320.00 in wages that year, minus the $3.20 trustees took out of her paycheck for the retirement fund. She didn't have to file a tax form; Congress ratified the 16th Amendment to the U.S. Constitution (income tax) in 1913. And Farber didn't vote for Democrat Wilson, Republican Taft, Socialist Eugene Debs or the Bull Moose Party's Roosevelt in the fall 1912 presidential election. She and millions of other American women weren't given the right to vote until 1920, when the 19th Amendment was adopted.

Farber's school calendar was 160 days long. Minus the five legal holidays, she actually taught 155 days that year.

There were 15 school-aged children (10 boys and five girls) living in the district at the time, but only 10 (six boys and four girls) were registered at the school.

As many students have learned in home economics class, warm temperatures activate yeast in bread dough during the proofing process, and the dough starts R-I-S-I-N-G. Yet when Farber spoke of the man who owned the school house land, she was talking about George R-E-I-S-I-N-G.

Americans are well-known for simplifying the spelling of foreign names, especially when immigrants were processed at places such as

The Rising District School, artifact No. 87.78

(Photo courtesy of the Adirondack Museum)

Ellis Island in the 19th and 20th centuries. Luckily, when George Reising's parents moved to the United States from Germany, their name was kept intact.

The school house built in 1907 on land owned by George and Florence Reising was originally known as the Reising School, yet it later became the Rising School. At the time, land donation for schools was a common practice where land was plentiful. The school was constructed in a remote part of the Herkimer County town of Ohio, just north of West Canada Creek, close to what is now Route 365.

Functioning until 1945, it never had running water or electricity, and a well on the Reising property supplied the water. Chemical toilets were installed in a shed addition after the school reopened in 1932. There were two toilets, one for the girls and one for the boys.

The Alphonso Annotto family donated the Rising School to the Museum in 1987, and it was moved to Blue Mountain Lake in the fall of that year. Black-and-white photos in the Adirondack Museum's archives tell the story of moving day.

The 19-by-25-foot structure was transported in two pieces, the first floor then the gable. Photos show the school house, without the roof, being moved on a flatbed tractor trailer and escorted by a patrol car. A sign stating "OVER SIZED LOAD" was attached to the front of the truck, and "wide load" was written on the side of the building. One photo shows a sheriff's deputy directing traffic at an intersection on Route 30.

When the school house pulled into an empty parking lot at the Adirondack Museum, a television crew was videotaping the arrival. The date on the back of the photo is November 1987.

The donation included an "Enterprise Oak" stove, six desk brackets, 14 desk tops and seats, a number board, 19 wall slates, a desk frame and a cloak room door. These, however, are not the original furnishings, and the artifacts inside the school house came from an assortment of donors, including other school districts.

The Rising District School was restored before it was unveiled to the public at the Aug. 13, 1989 dedication ceremony. The roof was rebuilt, and a toilet room was reattached. The exterior was painted white with green trim to match the original colors, and although the interior walls were washed, the paint was left untouched.

Asked why Museum officials were interested in acquiring the Rising District School, Adam Hochschild said the they wanted to "say something about and celebrate education in the Adirondacks," according to a 1989 Hamilton County News report. His father, Harold Hochschild, opened the Museum in 1957.

Chapter 30

Reuben Cary's camping utensils

I never thought I'd be looking at camp cookware once owned by the man who killed the last timber wolf in the Adirondacks.

The year was 1893, the man, Reuben Cary.

In any case, that particular story is not important here, unless he ate the last timber wolf in the Adirondacks with the knife-and-fork set we're examining today. The set is artifact No. 83.48 in the Adirondack Museum's collection (currently in storage).

Ninety years after the 1893 wolf killing, one of Cary's great-granddaughters donated 19 items in a tool chest once owned by the Long Lake guide. Among the items were scissors, a button hook, a tool kit, a whetstone, a folding pocket knife, a fishing knife, a bobbin, a measuring tool, a hunting knife, a razor, a rabbet plane, an awl, a stitching tool, a scribe, and a cobbler's hammer. The donation also includes a 4-foot long panoramic photograph of Brandreth Lake, where Cary was employed for many years.

The knife and fork are part of a metal camp set housed in a soft, leather sheath, green in color and faded from obvious use. Turning the knife upside down, the two utensils slide into each other like a puzzle. What's left is a thin, metal bar that hides the knife and fork, making it safer to travel with in the woods.

Cary was born about 1844 in the Hamilton County hamlet of Long Lake and was the oldest of five children, according to Charles Brumley's book, "Guides of the Adirondacks, a History: A Short Season, Hard Work, Low Pay." Cary's father, Thomas, was a Vermont-born farmer, and his mother, Jane, was a New York-born housewife, according to the 1850 Federal Census for the town of Long Lake (source: www.rootsweb.com).

In 1864, Cary headed into the forest on his first guiding trip, and he was hooked.

In 1874, famous Glens Falls photographer and guide book publisher Seneca Ray Stoddard, in his "The Adirondacks: Illustrated" guide book, named "Reuben Carey" [sic] and his younger brother Nelson as two of the 33 "superior guides of the kind called independent" in Long Lake. The list was not made in alphabetical order, and if Stoddard listed the guides from the best to worst, using No. 1 as the top guide, then the Cary brothers were highly regarded in the Long Lake guiding scene. "Mitchel Sabattis" [sic] was first and "John

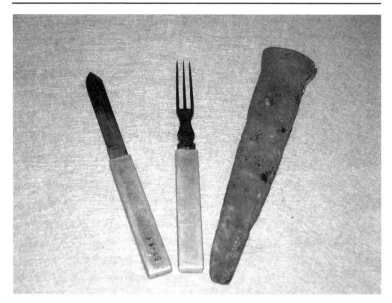

Adirondack guide Reuben Cary's camping knife and fork, artifact No. 83.48

(Photo courtesy of the Adirondack Museum)

Plumbley" [sic] second. Reuben was third and Nelson Cary fourth. The list was provided by C.H. Kellogg, Esq., of the Long Lake Hotel.

Reuben Cary guided a number of notable personalities in his day, including artist Arthur Fitzwilliam Tait, who had bought land and lived in the town of Long Lake, and he helped World War I Gen. John J. Pershing get a buck.

He worked for the Benedict family of New York City for several seasons and traveled with William Constable, of Constableville, on a salmon fishing trip to the Marguerite River in Canada. He also guided Steven Constable, James Blandford and Dr. Benjamin Brandreth.

In 1880, Reuben Cary began working for the Brandreth Park Reserve as gamekeeper and caretaker. He stayed there until 1930. Brandreth Lake, which is still privately owned, is located west of Long Lake, between Lake Lila to the north and Raquette Lake to the south.

A good portion of Adirondack guides, past and present, earn their living from a number of sources. Many in the 19th century were farmers and loggers and boat-builders. In 1877, Hallock's Gazetteer listed Reuben Cary, of Long Lake, as a guideboat builder. Hallock's called the watercraft an "Adirondack boat" and described it as a "round-bottom, lap streak cedar boat."

Hunting was an important part of the 19th century guide's job duties, and Reuben Cary hunted with a breech-loading Maynard rifle. According to Brumley's book, Cary was quoted as saying, "Arnold and Sam Dunnigan and Clark Farmer got 25 or 30 panther skins on a trip one winter down Brown's Tract—that's how panthers came to be exterminated."

Reuben Cary died in 1933 at age 89.

There's not much information available about Cary's knife-and-fork set, but it reminds me of the silverware set I owned as a Boy Scout—a knife, fork and spoon that latched together. They were housed in a hard, plastic sheath, green in color, dusty and faded from obvious use.

I originally found the set when I was about 12, in my basement with other camping items in a canvas Boy Scout backpack. It was my father's, and within months I was a Boy Scout, using the utensils on camping trips in the Tupper Lake area. I still have the dusty, green pack, the merit badges I earned, and the knife, fork and spoon—ready to be used once again by someone much younger.

Chapter 31

Ginseng harvesting tool

Harvesting American ginseng root has been an important part of New York's economy since the days of Gen. George Washington. It is believed that the general used proceeds from this cash crop to finance his army during the American Revolution. Today, it is a multimillion-dollar industry in this state alone.

Ginseng is rare and valuable, and its root is consumed for medicinal purposes. Therefore, it is the ginseng root that must be dug up, cleaned and shipped to destinations as far away as China.

The Adirondack Museum's ginseng harvester hand tool, artifact No. 2001.38.2 in the collection (currently in storage), was used in the latter half of the 19th century in New York state. Purchased from an antique dealer in the Franklin County village of Tupper Lake, the tool's origin and owner are unknown.

At 12 inches long, the ginseng harvester has a metal head at the end of a wooden handle, which was originally a chisel handle. The head has two functions: one side is flat for digging; the other side is forked for loosening dirt around the root. Ginseng root is most valuable if it is not broken.

At maturity, American ginseng is between 8 and 15 inches tall and can be identified by its three groups of green leaves and a cluster of red berries in the middle. Each group, or prong, has three large leaves at the top and two small ones at the bottom. The perennial plant grows in shaded areas of the forest and favors north- or east-facing slopes in rich, well-drained soil.

Wild ginseng has been heavily harvested throughout New York, including the Adirondacks. The Empire State Ginseng Growers Association represents local harvesters, and the state's industry is heavily regulated by the Department of Environmental Conservation. The state's ginseng business is conducted only on private property; it is illegal to harvest the root on state land. American ginseng is a federally endangered species, and the harvest is heavily regulated by state and federal governments in accordance with international trade standards.

In 1987, New York adopted regulations for the American ginseng, establishing a harvest season, a dealer permitting system, conservation practices and certification procedures.

"The ultimate goal of the ginseng program is to insure the survival of the species in the wild," the DEC states. "By providing technical

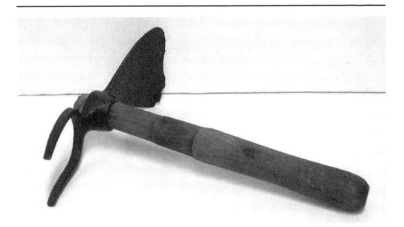

Tool used to harvest ginseng root, artifact No. 2001.38.2

(Photo courtesy of the Adirondack Museum)

assistance and information to ginseng growers, harvesters, and dealers, the DEC can help conserve the species, while providing jobs and income to many people."

The state's ginseng harvest starts on Sept. 1 and ends on Nov. 30, and the sale and purchase of green wild ginseng in the state is prohibited between Jan. 1 and Aug. 31. The DEC also prohibits the sale and purchase of dry ginseng during the growing season (April 1 - Sept. 15), unless previously weighed and recorded by the state by March 31.

Only mature wild ginseng plants may be harvested. The plants must have at least three five-leaflet prongs and ripe fruit. In addition, "all seeds from collected wild ginseng plants must be planted, in mineral soil to the depth of the thickness of the seed within 50 feet of the place of collection, immediately after collection," according to the DEC regulations. In 1988, the U.S. Department of the Interior, Fish and Wildlife Service approved the New York State American Ginseng Program. At the same time, it lifted a ban on the export of New York-grown ginseng.

A Jesuit priest originally discovered ginseng in this region in 1715. Today the DEC estimates that ginseng harvesting in the state grosses $3 million annually, and New York dealers buy and sell another $50 million of out-of-state ginseng each year.

The root can be consumed in many ways. It has been made into tea and wine, chewed raw and formed into life-invigorating pills.

Ginseng—the root of life—is said to revitalize the human body, boosting metabolism, decreasing blood pressure and improving the central nervous system.

Chapter 32

Fruit press (cider mill)

It's fun to think that drinking apple cider—that magic potion of autumn—can make people live longer.

While science may not support this fictional assessment, those who lived on the old Bennett farm in North River lived long and healthy lives. And we may never know if the homemade apple cider had anything to do with it.

If it did, the Adirondack Museum owns the fountain of youth—a small fruit press, or cider mill, from the Bennett farm on Rogers Road in the Warren County town of Johnsburg. It dates to between 1880 and 1900 and is artifact No. 67.142.77 in the Museum's collection (currently in storage).

Leonard Bennett was born around 1800 in Vermont and moved to North River in 1847 to settle with his wife and children, according to information provided by Johnsburg Town Historian Doris Patton. Bennett died on Jan. 17, 1874 at the age of 74, which was young compared to later generations.

Two of Bennett's sons, George and William, had sons of their own that directly relate to the cider mill, Leonard and Edwin, respectively. They were cousins, and it was Leonard's son, Kenneth, who gave the cider mill to the Museum in 1967 as part of Edwin Bennett's estate. Edwin Bennett was born on Jan. 9, 1866 in North River. He apparently never married, as there is no wife listed in his obituary. He died on Sept. 29, 1963 at the age of 97. His father lived to be 85.

The Adirondack Museum received hundreds of items from Edwin Bennett's farm. The first portion of the gift included the cider mill, a milking stool, beekeeping frames, a buggy whip, a hog scraper, a farrier's knife, and horse nails. Kenneth Bennett, who died in 1987 at the age of 91, was listed as the donor. Later items from the farm were given to the Museum by the Kaufmanns, the family that bought the Bennett property.

We don't know how much apple cider (sweet or hard) the Bennetts consumed on their farm or how often the cider mill was used, but we do know that the basic design of smaller fruit presses has changed little over the past 150 years.

This particular cider mill, a heavy and crude early model, is made of steel, iron and wood. The place of origin is unknown; the iron parts have manufacturer numbers, but no other manufacturer information or

A 19th century fruit press or cider mill, artifact No. 67.142.77, once used on a North River farm

(Photo courtesy of the Adirondack Museum)

patent dates are evident.

It is a single-drum cider mill and consists of a grinder, which reduced fruit to a pulpy mass or pomace, and the press, which squeezed out the juice. It is encased in an iron frame with four angle-iron legs that support the iron gears, crusher and press.

At the top is the grinder, a four-sided sheet-metal funnel, where fruit was ground. There is a crank handle on one side and the gears on the other, and a flywheel is adjacent to the gears. The funnel can be removed to give the press a wider range of movement.

Mounted next to the funnel is the press, on a long-threaded rod, which is moved by a handle at the top. It compressed the pomace into the bucket using a round wooden lid. A slatted wooden bucket collected the pomace, and the juice ran out the front.

Most apple cider made in New York state is pasteurized, or heated to 160 degrees for a few seconds to kill the bacteria, according to the New York Apple Association. Yet many prefer to drink cider that hasn't been treated.

Apple cider in the United States falls into two categories: "sweet" freshly pressed juice and a "hard" fermented alcoholic beverage. Hard cider is making a comeback worldwide and is a popular drink in European countries such as England and Spain. France is the world's largest cider-producing country.

As for the health benefits of apples, Cornell University food scientists recently found that the fruit has cancer-fighting qualities. But you have to eat the skin, too. Apple skin contains phytochemicals, and researchers say that eating 100 grams of apples, with the skin, provides total antioxidant and cancer-fighting activity equal to 1,500 milligrams of vitamin C.

To make your own apple cider at home, according to the "Joy of Cooking" cookbook, use a variety of three or more firm, ripe apples, blending the sweet with the acidic. "After putting apples through a cider mill or fruit press ... strain and put into hot, sterile jars. Process 30 minutes in hot-water bath at 185 degrees."

Chapter 33

Chatham Fanning Mill

During the late 19th and early 20th centuries, farmers who wanted to separate grain from chaff and dirt used a hand-cranked machine, a belly-high wooden box known as a fanning mill.

One such farmer in the Warren County town of Bolton trusted his Chatham Fanning Mill to produce clean grain. The mill—made of wood, iron and steel—is 46.25 inches tall, 33 inches wide and 55 inches deep. It dates from about 1900 to 1910 and was used on the Raymond farm in Bolton Landing.

The Chatham Fanning Mill, donated to the Adirondack Museum in June 1987, is one of dozens of farm machines owned by the facility, and it helps tell the story of farming in the Adirondack region. It is artifact No. 87.17 in the Museum's collection (currently in storage).

Fanning mills were also called winnowing-machines or seed cleaners, and this particular one was made in Detroit, Mich. by the Manson Campbell Co. Museum curators derived the date from an advertisement that was featured in C.H. Wendel's "Encyclopedia of American Farm Implements and Antiques." It shows a model of the Chatham Fanning Mill the company sold in 1904.

When clean grain reached the bottom of the mill, it could be collected by a bucket, or farmers could buy a chest-high "patented sack attachment" (as shown in the advertisement) to blow the product into 3-foot-tall sacks.

The Chatham Fanning Mills were colorful, and that puzzled Wendel, who wrote, "For reasons unknown, fanning mills were usually decorated with extensive pin-striping, plus stencils or decals, even when most farm machinery was losing that special appearance."

Although the red paint, stenciled lines and scrolls have faded on the Museum's fanning mill, the wording can still be read. The galvanized housing has the maker's mark in large print: "Chatham Mill, Mfd. By the Manson Campbell Co., Detroit, Mich." The machine is structurally stable and was cleaned by Museum staff after it was acquired. The wire screens are rusted and broken in many spots.

After the field crops (oats, etc.) were dry, farmers would use a large threshing machine to separate grain from the stem and chaff. According to the Living History Farms in Urbandale, Iowa, the grain, or seed, was kept for animal feed, and the leftover straw was used for animal bedding. For seeds that were saved for planting, farmers then

Chatham Fanning Mill, artifact No. 87.17, once used in Bolton Landing
(Photo courtesy of the Adirondack Museum)

used a fanning mill to "super clean" the grain.

Pictures of a fanning mill demonstration can be found on the Living History Farms Web site (www.lhf.org).

It only took one person to operate a fanning mill. The grain was dropped in the adjustable feed slot at the top, and it passed through a series of screens with different sized holes, from coarse to fine. This allowed the coarser impurities to pass out between the upper screens and the finer ones between the lower screens. In all, there were 11 screens: three large, six medium and two small. The large screens were placed in the bottom section, and the small and medium screens fit in the top.

As the farmer turned the crank, the paddle wheel (fan), encased in galvanized housing, rotated and created a blast of air while the screens shook from side to side.

The hopper funnel took the grain off from the other end, beneath the fan, and directed the feed material to the patented sacking attachment. The Living History Farms fanning mill demonstration page states that the grain "comes out of the machine into a bucket on the ground," yet the bucket is out of sight.

For maintenance purposes, there are doors on each side of the mill to access the fan gears, and there is a drawer at the bottom, accessible from either side.

Agriculture is a major part of New York's economy, and milk is the leading product in the state, according to the U.S. Department of Agriculture (USDA). About 25 percent of the state land area, 7.6 million acres, is used by New York's 37,500 farms. That's about the size of Maryland and Delaware combined or two Rhode Islands attached to the Adirondack Park.

Fanning mills were used for field crops, and a majority of New York's field crops are grown in support of the dairy industry. The most widely grown field crops are corn, oats and wheat, but soybeans are becoming more important. Compared to the rest of the 50 states, in 2002, New York placed 31st in wheat production, 21st in grain corn, 20th in soybeans, ninth in oats, and third in corn silage.

Chapter 34

Robinson single-shot rifle

We've all heard of the famous American rifle-making families—Winchester, Browning, Robinson.

Well maybe not Robinson, but in the early 1870s Adirondack-made Robinson rifles were a source of pride for the fledgling Adirondack Arms Company, of Plattsburgh. Orvill M. Robinson was the inventor, and he designed rifles so well that the Winchester Repeating Arms Company bought his patents in 1874.

Robinson rifles are prized among collectors since so few were made. The Adirondack Museum owns several of these firearms, but one is special—a single-shot rifle with a rolling block action. It is artifact No. 2001.29.1 in the Museum's collection (currently in storage).

The rifle was acquired from a couple in the Clinton County town of Plattsburgh who bought it from Robinson's great-grandson, Paul, "twenty-or-so years ago." That was in 2001. The firearm was almost sold to the Buffalo Bill Museum in Cody, Wyo., but the sellers approached the Adirondack Museum because they wanted it to stay in the region.

The rifle—made of wood, iron, nickel and brass—is 42.25 inches long. It is a single-shot, breech-loading rifle that fires a .44 caliber cartridge. The acquisition included a .44 caliber Henry rimfire bullet. The stock is made of walnut, and the barrel is steel. It has a front sight of brass, and the rear sight is a notched blade and adjustable pinhole. The rifle features a curved trigger guard, a lever that is used for ejecting the shell and closing the chamber. There are no markings.

The Adirondack Museum has owned two Robinson repeating rifles (Type II style), made during the 1870s by the Adirondack Arms Co., for many years. This single-shot rifle, however, was called "unusual" by a Museum curator because it is one of the last rifles Orvill Robinson made—one of only two single-shot rifles.

In 1864, Robinson moved from Highgate Center, Vt. to Lake Placid. That was before the West was won with Winchester's Model 1873 repeating rifle, even before the Union Army used the Springfield Model 1863 Rifle-Musket to defeat the Confederate Army in the Civil War. In 1867, Robinson moved to more spacious quarters in Upper Jay to hone his gunsmithing skills.

In 1870, Robinson patented an "Improvement in Breech-Loading Fire-Arms" with a unique repeating rifle action (which was refined in

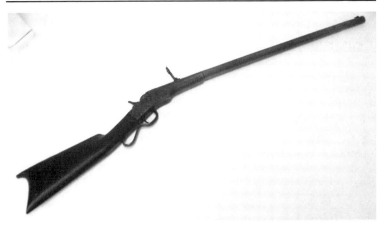

A single-shot rifle, artifact No. 2001.29.1, made by Orvill M.
Robinson around 1874

(Photo courtesy of the Adirondack Museum)

1872). The action was operated manually by sliding the breech bolt
back and forth horizontally.

Robinson's patented rifles were repeaters, and they were manufactured by the Adirondack Arms Company from about 1872 to 1874.
According to Mark Cross, author of the "Robinson Rifles" story in the
Northeast Arms Collector and Journal (Sept. 15, 1985), the inventor
made two single-shot rifles in 1874 or shortly thereafter before moving
out of the region.

Robinson's two single-shot rifles, including the Adirondack
Museum's, were featured in Paul Peck's Spring 1973 Adirondack Life
story, "The Adirondack Arms Company." Peck labels the rifle as a
"sporterized rolling block." Sporterized rifles are typically military
firearms that are modified for civilian hunting. "Rolling block" refers
to the action of the rifle, or how the cartridge gets locked in the chamber from the breech, or back of the barrel.

When the rifle's lever is operated, the block action (between the
hammer and the breech) rolls back and ejects the shell. A new cartridge can then be placed in the chamber. When the lever is returned to
its previous position, it rolls the block forward to the breech and locks
the action.

Another American gunsmith, Utah-based John Moses Browning,
made falling block action single-shot rifles, and his first patent met the
same fate as Robinson's. Like many late 19th century capitalist giants,
the Winchester Repeating Arms Company gobbled up the competition
by taking over companies and buying patents around the U.S., includ-

ing Robinson's repeating rifles in 1874 and Browning's first single-shot rifle in 1883.

Browning's bliss was invention, not manufacturing, so he began working for Winchester and by the time he died in 1926, he had created some of the most popular and innovative guns in American history, including the Winchester Model 1886 lever action repeating rifle, the Winchester Model 1887 lever action repeating shotgun, the Colt Model 1895 Peacemaker machine-gun and the Browning Automatic Rifle (BAR).

When Robinson moved out of the Adirondacks, to Penn Yan and then St. Paul, he gave up the gunsmith trade and became a wheelwright and accomplished violin maker. His family, however, preserved his Adirondack roots.

Robinson's son, William, returned to Upper Jay and opened a wagon-making and wheelwright business. William's son, Walter, continued the family business and made furniture. Walters' son, Paul, operated a service station in Upper Jay that included a hardware store and gunsmith shop. Paul Robinson supplied much of the information for Peck's Adirondack Life story.

Chapter 35

Utica Duxbak hunting coat and pants

Rain can make any hunting, fishing or outdoor trip miserable. Luckily, throughout most of the 20th century, sportsmen could rely on comfortable and stylish clothing made by the Utica Duxbak Corporation, a North Country business that produced world-famous jackets, pants and vests.

Ironically, this company found inspiration from an animal its customers would eventually kill—the duck.

Duxbak "Sheds Water Like a Duck's Back." That was the motto, and it worked.

Ducks have an oil gland on their back at the base of the upper tail, and they use their bills to spread the oil from the gland onto their feathers, making them waterproof. As their heads stretch backward, they "preen" or comb the back feathers to keep them clean and well oiled.

Since equipping sportsmen with oil glands was not an option, Utica Duxbak relied on its own waterproofing method, the Priestly Cravenette Process, "which we control exclusively in the United States for hunting garments," the company stated in its Nov. 14, 1908 advertisement in Forest and Stream magazine.

"The only hunting garments giving thorough comfort in all weathers. Soft as chamois and tailored to a perfect fit." The advertisement shows a woman holding a shotgun while standing in a boat and a man aiming a gun at the reader.

"Duxbak Sportsmen's clothing allows perfect ventilation, insures long, hard wear, and a dressy appearance under all conditions. Fit and waterproof qualities guaranteed. Two colors only—light tan and olive green."

For the gentlemen, the advertisement listed its wares: a regular hunting coat, Norfolk jacket, long trousers, knickerbockers, riding trousers, hats, caps, vests and leggings. For the ladies, it offered a regular hunting coat, Norfolk jacket, plain skirt, divided skirt, bloomers, leggings and hats "suitable for gunning, fishing, riding, tramping, boating or climbing."

In 1908, women were still fairly new to the world of outdoor recreation, hunting in particular, yet there were exceptions. In the age of an ever-growing women's suffrage movement, more and more independently minded American women were arming themselves with

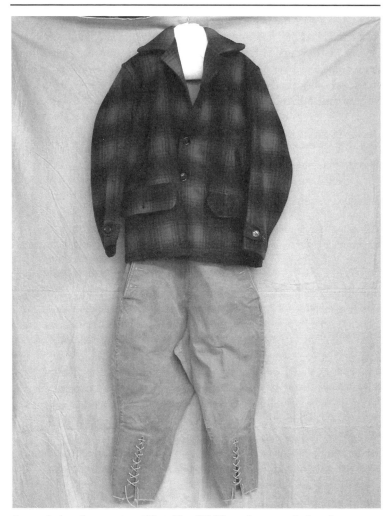

A men's hunting coat, artifact No. 87.69, and women's hunting pants, artifact No. 93.35, made by Utica Duxbak Corporation

(Photo courtesy of the Adirondack Museum)

guns and grit and heading to the backcountry to hunt white-tailed deer and waterfowl. They couldn't vote, but they could kill a duck or two. In a roundabout way, Edward Buck wrote about this phenomenon in his 1908 book, "The Way of the Woods," published by Putnam's Sons in New York. He gave "Tips for Women" and wrote about the male sportsmen who refused to be "bothered by women-folks in camp."

"The important thing to cultivate is independence," Buck wrote.

"Let the men of the party once discover that the lady does not require to be mollicoddled [sic] or waited on all day long and that she is a 'good sport,' which is another way of saying that she takes everything as it comes, and her path will be easy, as well as that of her male companions. But from the nervous woman, or the petulant one, or her who screams at sight of a mouse or an innocent daddy-longlegs—good Lord deliver us! It is mostly a matter of that first of social qualities, tact. Blessed is she who is helpful without screaming to interfere; happy is she who is not afraid that her hands will roughen, her feet grow broad, and her crow's feet deepen."

Buck also suggested the following camping clothes for ladies: full Duxbak or khaki suit with "fairly short skirt," extra cloth skirt, brown or dark grey knickerbockers, silk neckerchief, and canvas leggings. He also said they should be equipped with underwear, shirts, stockings, headgear, gloves (pair of thick chamois), footwear, toilet-articles, medicines, specialties and "waterproofs."

The Adirondack Museum owns many Duxbak clothing items, such as this week's artifacts, a 1940s men's wool "Drybak" red and plaid hunting coat (No. 87.69) and a pair of 1930s women's hunting pants (No. 93.35). They are currently in storage in the Museum's collection.

The pants were part of a three-piece women's hunting outfit donated in 1993. The donor found it in her 85-year-old mother's things and said, "I know she could never have worn it," referring to the small size of the clothes (32-inch waist skirt and 30-inch waist pants). Her mother had apparently collected it from another source.

The brown outfit is made of canvas and includes a jacket and skirt with bone buttons and a set of single-layer pants with tapered legs. The calf-length pants have calf lacings, four-button (metal) side openings, one rear pocket and two suspender buttons inside the front waist. The skirt label reads, "Duxbak, Trade Mark, Rain Proof, Sportsman's clothing, Utica Duxbak Corp, Utica NY."

The men's clothing, dating from the pre-1920s to the 1940s, was donated by the Utica Duxbak Corporation in 1987 when the company was going out of business. Based on a suggestion from the Oneida Historical Society, Utica Duxbak President Gilbert Jones sent men's and women's clothing, patents, catalogs and 16-by-26-inch pictures to the Adirondack Museum.

He spoke of the Duxbak demise in a Nov. 10, 1987 letter to the Museum. Jones somberly wrote, "The Duxbak name has been sold and Utica Duxbak Corporation is going out of business." It was written on official company letterhead, decorated with the symbol of Duxbak prosperity—the logo of a duck.

Beam knife used for murder

Edward Earl's recipe for murder called for a knife, a wife, opportunity and motive. Take some infidelity, vengeance, add a dash of rage. Stir the pot, and let the ingredients brew.

"Murder is a terrible word," Earl wrote in his 1881 confession. "I could never hear that word spoken without associating it with something awful ... Oh, God! It was horrible indeed."

Yes, Earl killed his wife, but maybe he was destined to die with a hangman's noose around his neck, banished for eternity to the far end of the Hope Falls Cemetery. After all, his never-ending quest for love was anything but boring. It led him to the West Coast, around the tip of South America, and to the heart of Dixie before grief and whiskey washed away his dreams in the backwoods of southern Hamilton County.

Edward Earl was born in 1840 in Virginia. An only child, his mother died when he was 8 years old, and he was later sent to Annapolis, Md. to attend school.

Restless, he moved to the Hamilton County town of Benson in 1858, where he sought a new life, a new identity. Earl fell in love with a young lady in Benson, Harriet Hall, who repeatedly denied his advances. Giving up on love for the moment, he moved to California, where he worked in the mining industry. He shipped to Havana and then to Charleston, S.C., where he was captured by the Confederate Army and jailed as an alleged Union spy for 15 months. During Major-Gen. William T. Sherman's famous "March to the Sea" in 1864, Earl and other prisoners were liberated when their Rebel guards fled.

After his release, Earl returned to Hamilton County and found that Harriet Hall had married "his rival," Dewitt Wright. With no chance at winning Hall's heart, he moved to the village of Kingsboro in Fulton County and worked as a farm laborer for Duncan McGregor. During this period, he gave himself an alias, Edward H. Poindexter.

By the fall of 1865, Earl was living in the southern Hamilton County hamlet of Hope Falls, calling himself Edward Earl again, according to the 1881 pamphlet, "The Life, Confession, Writings and Execution of Edward Earl." He worked as a blacksmith for Smith & Ressigue, tanners and lumbermen, and when work was slow he "kept shanty" for a lumberman named George Brown, who lived near the Warren County line.

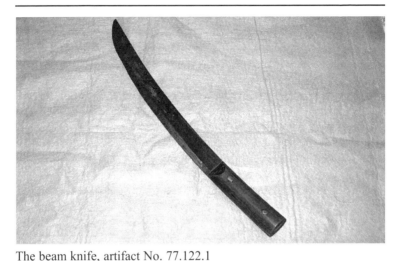

The beam knife, artifact No. 77.122.1

(Photo courtesy of the Adirondack Museum)

Earl soon met and courted Mary Burgess, a teenager who "was born and reared in the wilds of Hamilton County, uneducated, mentally and morally, and whose only charms consisted in her red cheeks, ruby lips, elastic step and healthy appearance," the 1881 pamphlet states. The couple married in the town of Hope in October 1868 and had three children, two girls and a boy. Their son and first daughter died young and were buried in the Hope Falls Cemetery. Their surviving daughter, June, was born in June 1875.

Their marriage was rocky, to say the least, "Edward taking again to the cursed intoxicating beverage (whiskey), Mary to the embrace of the illiterate Bill Hall," the 1881 pamphlet states. They separated in 1877 when Mary left him for his seasonal employer, George Brown. During an argument shortly after the separation, Edward pleaded for Mary to return home. She refused. Before long, a Fulton County grand jury had indicted him for assaulting his wife with a knife. Although she didn't suffer any wounds and he protested his innocence, Edward was convicted and sent to the Dannemora state prison, where he swore vengeance during his three-and-a-half-year sentence.

Edward was released on Nov. 19, 1880. He killed his wife on Feb. 19, 1881.

If Edward Earl couldn't have his wife back, he could at least try to gain custody of their 5-year-old daughter, who was living with Mary at Brown's farm. On Feb. 14, he went to Brown's house to beg for the child but was denied. Edward returned several days later and confronted her in the barn.

The portraits of Edward Earl, taken after his conviction, and Mary Earl, taken two days before her murder, were printed on the 1881 pamphlet, "The Life, Confession, Writings and Execution of Edward Earl."

(Photo courtesy of the Adirondack Museum)

Edward hid in a pile of hay, which Mary was using to feed the animals, and approached her. Startled, she lunged at him with a pitchfork. He disarmed her and wielded a beam knife to get her attention. Edward had stolen the 16-inch-long knife from his employers, Smith & Ressigue. The knife, with a 13-inch-long and 2-inch-wide blade, is artifact No. 77.122.1 in the Adirondack Museum's collection (currently in storage). A beam knife is used for fleshing out hides at tanneries, and this one was probably made from the end of a scythe blade.

Seeing that Edward had a knife, Mary knelt before him and pleaded for her life. He desperately wanted revenge for putting him in prison, but Mary had a way with words.

"I threw the knife on the floor at her feet, went to the door, went out," Edward said in his confession (Sept. 10, 1881). "I stood beside the door, undecided—stupid.

"Where could I go? I had no object in life now—the hope of vengeance that had kept me alive for years had been wrested from me by the earnest pleadings of the woman."

Mary promised to keep the incident quiet, but when she thought he had left the barn, she rushed to the door and yelled, "George! George!"

Fearing another prison sentence, Edward snapped.

"Her present treachery maddened me beyond all control," he wrote in the confession. "I was no longer human. I was a demon, knowing nothing; fearing nothing—wild!"

He ran through the barn, and she tripped in the door and fell.

"I snatched the knife from her hand, and, did I strike? No. It was the years of suffering, woe, shame, dishonor, the desolate home, justice, and the hated name of George that held the knife and impelled the blow, as she shrieked—murder!"

Edward drove the knife into Mary's chest and severed every artery leading to and from her heart.

"I stared in stupid horror for a moment, then like a wild beast fled across the field, the fearful cry of murder ringing in my ears ... I raised my hands to my ears to shut out the awful sounds and became conscious that my hand grasped something. Horror on horror, it was a knife covered with blood. I hurled it from me and as it fell it shrieked murder."

Edward immediately surrendered himself to the authorities in Northville and was taken to the Hamilton County Jail on Feb. 20, 1881. The jail was located at the county seat in Sageville, which is now part of the hamlet of Lake Pleasant.

Edward was indicted in June and convicted in August. On the morning of Oct. 14, 1881, about 1,000 people packed Sageville. The hanging yard, 48 by 58 feet, was between the jail and the courthouse. Sheriff Patrick Mitchell led Edward up the scaffold, placed the rope around his neck, and pinioned his arms and legs. After a few final remarks, Edward said, "Sheriff, I am ready. Good-bye all."

With that, Mitchell drew a black cap over the convict's face and sprung the trap of the gallows at 11:35 a.m. Edward Earl was dead by 11:44 and placed in his coffin at 11:47.

Edward and Mary are both buried in the Hope Falls Cemetery, but not together, according to "The History of Hamilton County," written by Ted Aber and Stella King. Edward was placed near the back of the cemetery, upon the request of Mary's father. Such is the fate of the Hamilton County Murderer.

The story of the knife, however, does not end with Edward's interment.

Dr. Clarence Blake, the doctor at the trial, kept the murder weapon and later used it to cut up cabbage for his chickens. The knife was then owned by his son, Harry Blake, and Nelson Dunham, the attorney who settled Harry Blake's estate. Dunham gave the knife to the Northville man who donated it to the Adirondack Museum.

Chapter 37

Bonnie Belle Farm acetylene generator

Early risers hail the end of Daylight Savings Time as a much-needed extra hour of light, though gloomy this time of year. Workers, rushing home at 5 o'clock, feel the burden of darkness weighing on their weary souls. If you listen closely, when they return home, you can hear the flipping of light switches and sighs of relief reverberate through the mountain valleys and river corridors. Light is expected here, taken for granted in the 21st century.

In history classes, stories are told about candles and kerosene lamps being used for household illumination. They conjure up visions of Abraham Lincoln reading by firelight and reruns of "Little House on the Prairie." But we rarely hear about the acetylene years.

There was a time, starting in the 1890s, that people used acetylene gas to generate light in their homes. That was before electric grids crisscrossed the American landscape. Other parts of the U.S. and the world used natural gas during this transition period, but that was not an option in the Adirondack Mountains.

Many Great Camp owners and other seasonal residents purchased acetylene generators, or gas plants, for their Adirondack homes. They were expensive, heavy and dangerous. Yet the results were well-worth the purchase cost and risk of fire; acetylene, when burned in lamps, was far brighter than lighting available at the time. The flame, when burned with oxygen, was 1,000 degrees Celsius hotter than any other, according to the American Chemical Society.

That's probably why Mr. Snow, of New York City, had an acetylene generator installed in his large, summer home near Loon Lake in Warren County. The gas plant—made of steel, iron and copper—is artifact No. 74.209 in the Adirondack Museum's collection (currently in storage). It dates to between 1895 and 1905.

The generator basically looks like two chest-high, metal drums standing side-by-side, connected by pipes. The drum on the left, slightly taller, has a metal hopper on the top. The entire contraption is 66 inches tall, 56 inches wide, 30 inches deep, and the drums are 23 inches in diameter. It was made by the J.B. Colt Company, possibly in Buffalo.

C. Albert Jacob bought Snow's seasonal property in 1905 and named it Bonnie Belle Farm after his wife. In 1966, C. Albert Jacob Jr., of Scarsdale, wrote to the Adirondack Museum in the hope of

The acetylene generator, artifact No. 74.209, once used at the Bonnie Belle Farm near Loon Lake in Warren County

(Photo courtesy of the Adirondack Museum)

donating the generator and a hanging lamp to the collection. Most of the original lamps were long gone by that time.

"When we went over from gas to electricity, we had dozens of gas fixtures that were stored in the barn," Jacob Jr. wrote. "They were all solid brass fixtures, and when World War II came along and the scrap metal drives were instituted, we had an attack of patriotism and turned them all in. I wonder now that the generator and this one lamp survived, but they did and I'm happy to know they'll find a home at Blue Mountain."

By the time the gas plant was picked up in 1974, Jacob's granddaughter, of Chestertown, was listed as the donor. In correspondence with the Museum, she explained where it was used on the property. Unlike some homeowners who kept acetylene gas plants in their cellars, the Bonnie Belle Farm generator was stored 200 yards from the house, in a kind of root cellar or bunker that was constructed in the side of a hill. The housing was made of poured concrete, decorated with field stone in the front, and equipped with heavy double doors.

"I assume they were concerned about explosions from the gas plant and wanted it away from the house," she wrote. "We always heard that unless the gas machine was kept reasonably clean that there was a danger of malfunction and then an explosion or fire."

The plant generates acetylene (C_2H_2) by combining calcium carbide powder (CaC_2) with water. It consists of two parts connected by a pipe. The barrel on the left is used for the generation of gas, and the other is a holding tank for the pressurized gas.

The generator barrel includes a funnel-shaped reservoir on top that is loaded with carbide powder. The powder had been purchased from the Union Carbide Company, which was formed in 1898 to manufacture calcium carbide for acetylene lighting and is now a subsidiary of the DOW Chemical Company.

The label on the front of the generator reads "Colt Trademark, Acetylene Gas Generator, JB Colt Co." The top states, "Important: Change all water whenever any carbide is put in." The white powder caked on the outside of the tank is aqueous calcium dihydroxide $Ca(OH)_2(aq)$, the byproduct of the reaction.

The second barrel, a collapsible holding tank, held the acetylene gas in one barrel called the "the bell," which floated in water inside. The water was used as a seal to prevent the gas from escaping. The inside barrel could rise 10 inches to increase the capacity of gas. The tank includes a blow-off pipe and a service pipe to deliver the gas to the house.

Chapter 38

Barn loom

What's in your attic?

When a Glens Falls couple purchased a summer camp in the Warren County hamlet of North River, they found an antique barn loom in the loft.

A barn loom, mind you, is no small stack of firewood. They were called barn looms in the 19th century because some were erected in barns, although others were set up in homes and on porches. They were constructed so they could be taken apart and stored for the winter, many times in barns or sheds.

The couple donated the North River loom to the Adirondack Museum in 1974. It is artifact No. 74.188 in the Museum's collection (currently in storage).

The loom, which dates between 1820 and 1870, is made of wood and iron. It is 73 inches tall, 60 inches wide and 80 inches deep. It was used to make heavy cloth with homespun wool.

"Anecdotal evidence indicates that the original owner was a retired textile manufacturer from Long Island who collected antiques," states the barn loom's accession file. "It had been on the property for at least 50 years."

The loom was originally bought in Keeseville or Plattsburgh. In 1975, it was reassembled at the Adirondack Museum by a volunteer with weaving experience.

This particular loom has also been called a "bench loom," which features a built-in bench at the front of the machine. An extension has been added to the loom for comfort. Otherwise, the weaver's rear end would have been hanging off the wood beam used as the seat. Hours of weaving could have been torture without this modification.

Designed after a basic European style, the loom was constructed with a mortise-and-tenon wooden frame with pegs. This allowed the owner to disassemble the loom when it was not in use.

"The two-harness loom has a large warp beam, string heddles, a reed beater in a swing frame, or batten, and two treadles," the loom's file states. "The harnesses are suspended from two handmade wooden pulleys. The cloth beam, which holds the woven textile taut and is located in front of the bench, has an iron cog or ratchet on one end and is held by an iron clutch bar."

Accessories that came with the donation include four reeds. One is on the loom.

Barn loom, artifact No. 74.188, found in a camp in North River
(Photo courtesy of the Adirondack Museum)

Unfortunately, this barn loom is in storage on Adirondack Museum property and cannot be seen by the general public. There are, however, barn looms on display at other museums throughout the Northeast, including Vermont and the Adirondack region.

South of the Adirondack Park, the Newark Valley Historical Society in Tioga County (northeast of Binghamton) offers a unique program at the Bement-Billings Farmstead. The Shuttles and Spindles Guild operates a weaving room at the museum that features a dozen looms, including a restored barn loom. The Guild is "dedicated to preserving the skills of spinning and weaving."

Closer to home, the Alice T. Miner Museum in Chazy has a fully functioning barn loom on display, and there are barn looms at the Shoreham Historical Society in Shoreham, Vt., and the Shelburne Museum in Shelburne, Vt.

There are more than 30 spinning guilds throughout New York state, including the Southern Adirondack Spinsters Guild in Hudson Falls, the Thousand Island Handspinners Guild in Cape Vincent, the Leatherstocking Spinners in Booneville and the Seaway Valley Spinners and Knitters in Massena. The president of the Adirondack Mountain Spinners in Crown Point uses a barn loom for projects in his studio.

Chapter 39

Arts and Crafts style highchair

'Tis the season to give thanks for what we have in life, and what we have in the Adirondack Park is a natural treasure—one that is simple and beautiful; one that fosters creativity, health and good living; one that is spiritual and organic.

Perhaps this is why craftsmen and artists of all disciplines call the Adirondacks home. It's their mountain muse. The abundance of natural materials and the appreciation for quality, handmade products help cultivate a cottage industry of arts and crafts in the Adirondack North Country region.

Those who buy and use Adirondack products feel an instant connection to the area. They know that if it's Adirondack-made, it's wholesome and clean. (No animals were injured in the making of this column.)

While the Adirondack region is a perfect breeding ground for artists who remain faithful to the American Arts and Crafts Movement of the late 19th and early 20th centuries, a good portion of today's Adirondack-made furniture is constructed by amateur woodworkers. The independent spirit of Adirondack do-it-yourselfers is alive and well in basements, garages and woodshops from Glens Falls to Plattsburgh.

Yet the history of this week's Adirondack Museum artifact, a wooden highchair, is a mystery. It may have been made by a professional Adirondack crafter or by someone's dad or grandpa for the newest addition to the family.

The highchair, which dates to between 1900 and 1925, was donated by a man from Blue Mountain Lake. It was probably used in the Warren County village of North Creek, according to the artifact's accession file. Otherwise, little is known about this piece of furniture, artifact No. 66.73 in the Museum's collection (currently in storage).

The highchair is 3 feet tall, 16.5 inches wide and 18.5 inches deep. It was made for an infant or small child, and all four legs rest on a base with a double cross-brace. The chair back is made from extensions of diagonal braces on the chair sides.

When buying a highchair in today's market, safety is a paramount concern. Consumer experts warn buyers to make sure the waist and crotch restraints are not attached to the tray. The buckle on the waist strap should be easy to use, and the tray should lock securely.

A highchair, artifact No. 66.73, made in the Arts and Crafts style

(Photo courtesy of the Adirondack Museum)

What tray? What restraints? That's one of the first things Museum workers noticed about this highchair; it has no restraints to prevent the child from falling out of the seat.

Looking at the well-worn seat and footrest, the highchair was obviously used many times. The parents must have watched the child very closely.

This highchair was made in the Arts and Crafts style. Made of wood, it has a simple design and is stained brown.

The Arts and Crafts Movement began in England in the mid-1800s to protest the mechanized production of goods during the Industrial Revolution, and it had social overtones that reverberated throughout the United Kingdom and United States until the 1920s. The resulting style found its way into many disciplines: furniture, pottery, architecture, interior design, even gardening.

Men such as William Morris and John Ruskin, both of England, rejected machine-produced goods and preached that industrialization was detrimental to the mental and physical health of workers.

"It is right and necessary that all men should have work to do which should be worth doing and be itself pleasant to do; and which should not be done under such conditions as would make it neither overwearisome nor overanxious," William Morris wrote.

Craftsmen who made products free of machines brought dignity to labor, Morris and Ruskin asserted. It made them honest and improved their quality of life. It gave the products integrity. It preserved traditional methods of craftsmanship.

The contemporary Arts and Crafts Movement in the Unites States is still being defined. It is dictated by geography ("Made in the Adirondacks" versus "Made in China") and influenced by our increasing need to escape from the microchip jungle.

It's time to shed the cell phone and laptop and MP3 player and give thanks for the simple pleasures in life—an Adirondack-made whatever, in this case, a highchair.

Chapter 40

'Grand Gold Coin' range stove

Many Americans will cook their holiday suppers this year with gas, electric or microwave stoves. Wood-burning cook stoves, for the most part, are a thing of the past, yet some are still being used in rural homes across the country.

At the turn of the 20th century, gas and electric stoves had been invented, but wood-fired cook stoves and ranges were still widely used. One of the country's leading stove-producing cities was Troy, N.Y.

A 1907-patented "Grand Gold Coin" wood-burning range stove is part of the Adirondack Museum's collection (currently in storage). It is artifact No. 56.46.4. Made of iron, steel and nickel, it was built by the Bussey & McLeod Stove Co. in Troy between 1907 and 1910, and the iron used in production may have come from mining operations in the Adirondack Mountains. It is 68.5 inches tall, 53 inches wide and 31 inches deep.

The stove is basically made of iron, with nickel-plated ornaments. It has four legs, a nickel grill shelf under the oven door, and a nickel pedal door opener under the right corner of oven door. The iron door has a nickel ornament in the center with the mark of Grand Gold Coin in the design.

The door on the right side of the front leads to the fire box, and the fire box door has a sliding vent and a Grand Gold Coin marking with 1907 on the front. There are six stove lids on the range and two detachable circular nickel warming grills on both sides of the stove pipe.

Not much is known about the past owners of this Grand Gold Coin stove or where it was used. It was purchased and given to the Adirondack Museum by a donor from Inwood, Long Island. While there may not be a direct connection to the Adirondack Mountains, this stove represents a way of life in America at the turn of the 20th century. Since it was built in Troy, Grand Gold Coin stoves were most likely used in the Adirondack North Country region at that time.

Information about the stove's manufacturer, Bussey & McLeod Stove Co., was published in 1891 by William H. Young in the book, "Troy's One Hundred Years: 1789-1889," compiled by Arthur James Weise. Excerpts on the "Manufacture of Stoves" chapter were found on the Rensselaer County NYGenWeb site on www.rootsweb.com.

A 1907-patented "Grand Gold Coin" wood-burning range stove, artifact
No. 56.46.4, made by the Bussey & McLeod Stove Co. in Troy.

(Photo courtesy of the Adirondack Museum)

The manufacture of stoves began in Troy in 1818, when the first foundry was built. By 1828, there were two foundries. By 1855, seven foundries manufactured stoves with a collective value of $1 million, and the five Troy foundries in 1888 cast stoves worth a total of $2 million.

"The conspicuous plant of the Bussey & McLeod Stove Company covers a plat of four acres on the east side of Oakwood Avenue, north of Hoosick Street," states the book by Weise. "The buildings, mostly four-story brick structures, command a wide view of the city and the Upper Hudson valley."

The Bussey, McLeod & Co.—formed by Esek Bussey, Charles A. McLeod and John O. Merriam—constructed its first buildings in 1863. The Bussey & McLeod Stove Company succeeded the firm on Dec. 30, 1882, with Esek Bussey, president; Charles A. McLeod, vice president; Esek Bussey Jr., treasurer; and Sayre McLeod, secretary.

The nickel-plated ornamentation and extra features on Bussey & McLeod stoves were seen as marketing assets.

"The thousands of stoves and ranges made at the works have many attractive features of construction and ornamentation which widely popularize the productions of the company in the eastern and western United States," Weise wrote.

Chapter 41

Dolls from the 1920s

In the eyes of the young, dolls can certainly become part of the family. A little girl from Castorland, for example, loved her three dolls so much she named each one after her mother, Rose Elizabeth.

The girl didn't have a separate bed for her dolls, so she used her father's. When she played house and it was time for their naps, she laid them down on his bed. Her father took them out of bed at night so he could go to sleep.

The three dolls and accessories were donated to the Adirondack Museum in 1996. The dolls were purchased for the donor when she was 10 to 12 years old, around 1920 to 1922, from the W.J. Snyder General Store, also known as the Center Store, in Castorland. Some of the clothes and accessories were handmade by her mother.

Castorland is located on the western shore of the Black River, in the Lewis County town of Denmark. The hamlet, north of Lowville and south of Carthage, is in the middle of farm country, just west of the Adirondack Park boundary.

The doll with the pink dress (artifact No. 96.46.3) is the oldest and was purchased around 1920. The largest doll (No. 96.46.1) with brown hair was her second, and the blonde-haired doll (No. 96.46.2) was her third, purchased around 1922.

The pink cotton dress on the smaller brunette is not original; new clothing was added when the doll was refurbished in the 1980s. It has a composition head and hands with moveable blue eyes, a closed mouth, a cloth body, and jointed hips and shoulders. The wig, which was added with the new set of clothes, features long, brown hair ringlets. The doll is wearing a full slip, a white half-slip, drawers, white cotton stockings, white imitation leather shoes, and two hair pins trimmed with a pink satin bow. At 16.5 inches tall, it is in good condition, but the right hand is cracked.

The largest doll has a composition head and hands, a cloth body, an open mouth, jointed legs, moveable eyes and straight brunette hair. The clothes were made by the donor's mother. The doll is wearing a muslin bonnet, a white muslin dress with lace, a white cotton full slip, a diaper, white cotton stockings, white wool booties, a gold heart-shaped pendant on a gold chain, a silver bar pin with purple and white enamel, and a pink-and-white crocheted wool sweater. At 23 inches tall, the doll is in good condition, even though it had been left out in the rain.

Dolls (artifacts No. 96.46.2, No. 96.46.3 and No. 96.46.1) purchased in the early 1920s in Castorland

(Photo courtesy of the Adirondack Museum)

The blonde-haired doll has composition hands, a cloth body, an open mouth, moveable blue eyes, and jointed shoulders, elbows, hips and knees. The head is made of bisque, a form of unglazed china. The doll is dressed in clothes made by the donor's mother: a white muslin bonnet, a white cotton dress, a white cotton full slip, a chemise, drawers, an undershirt, black cotton stockings, black suede boots, and a white wool crocheted sweater. At 22 inches tall, it is in good condition, and the hair is matted. On the back of the neck, just below the hair, is the name "ELIZABETH" written in cursive pencil. Made in Germany by Armand Marseille, the doll was a model 370, which was popular at the time. The maker's mark is also on the back of the neck.

The donation included several doll accessories, such as a feather pillow and cotton cases (artifacts No. 96.46.5 a-c) probably made by the donor's mother. There is a pink knit cap (No. 96.46.7) with a pompom on the top, circa 1970; a 22-inch-long pink, hand-knit scarf (No. 96.46.8), circa 1970; and a 14-inch-long flannel half-slip (No. 96.46.9) with a plain cotton waistband, circa 1920.

When I was ready to photograph the dolls, I put white gloves on my hands and carefully took the artifacts out of their boxes, which had been stored in a humidity- and temperature-controlled room. I soon found that standard point-and-shoot photography wouldn't work for this project. The models were uncooperative.

After placing the dolls gently on the counter, their eyes all shut at once. "Help!" I said, exerting minor frustration. Doreen Alessi came to the rescue (as always). She grabbed a white blanket, folded it and placed it underneath the gray backdrop. We propped the dolls up by sitting them on the gray lump. "Smile!" Snap. Snap. It was over in 5 seconds.

When the brief photo session in the Museum's office space ended, it was back to the boxes for these Castorland dolls. Back to storage, back to sleep.

Chapter 42

Artificial buffalo lap robes

When cars, or horse-less carriages, were first invented, the heater was not a top priority. Many of the first models were open-air carriages and required existing technology for heating their human passengers. Bundle up, baby, it's cold outside.

Lap robes were the technology of the day. They were blankets or fur pieces used to cover passengers, from the waist down, in unheated cars or horse-drawn carriages and sleighs. Some of the fur was real and some was synthetic.

The Adirondack Museum owns a collection of lap robes from the late 19th and early 20th centuries, including real and faux buffalo hide lap robes, also known as buffalo robes. Today we look at two imitation buffalo robes that were once used in the Adirondack region.

One of the buffalo robes, which the donor referred to as a "sleigh robe," came from the Hillcrest Farm "on Big Tupper Lake" in Franklin County. Donated in 1970, it is artifact No. 70.132 in the Museum's collection (currently in storage).

"It has been packed in a trunk—all these years," the donor said in a 1970 letter to the Museum staff. The letterhead was printed with the old phone number—154-J—which was crossed out and corrected in blue ink with the 1970 number, featuring the 359 prefix.

The robe was originally purchased in the early 1900s when the only means of transportation in the Adirondacks was by horse-drawn vehicles. It is made of brown poodle cloth (woven wool) and has green and blue felt trim. The back side is darker, rough brown wool, and there are tape loops on the upper back corners. It is in fair condition.

The other imitation buffalo robe, artifact No. 56.33, arrived before the Adirondack Museum opened in 1957. Construction was well under way, and the donor received a well-appreciated sneak peek of the Blue Mountain Lake facility.

"I am mailing you today the buffalo robe, less head and tail. Trust you may find some use for it," William Hill wrote on May 16, 1956. "[I] got a real thrill out of your project, particularly the dioramas." The correspondence was written on letterhead from Newton & Hill, distributors of machinery, hardware, mill supplies and Du Pont explosives in the Washington County village of Fort Edward.

The Feb. 27, 1957 thank-you note from former Adirondack Museum Director Robert Bruce Inverarity gives a glimpse into the

Artificial buffalo robe, artifact No. 70.132, once used in Tupper Lake
(Photo courtesy of the Adirondack Museum)

hectic process of creating a regional museum. He apologized for not sending the letter sooner.

"During the developmental stages of this Museum, many important phases are neglected or overlooked, not through desire but merely due to the pressure and large number of details involved," Inverarity wrote. "May I thank you on behalf of the Adirondack Museum of the Adirondack Historical Association for your generosity in giving us the buffalo robe."

The robe was made by the American Buffalo Robe Co., Howell Street, in Buffalo, N.Y. It dates between 1880 and 1920. It is rectangular and made of dark brown poodle cloth on both sides, and the fringe consists of a lighter brown felt. The front has a plush or velour surface and the back is looped to look like curly fur. The robe is lined with a stiff material, probably rubber to make it waterproof, a common feature with buffalo robes. The label on the back, near the edge, states: "American Buffalo Robe Co./Buffalo, N.Y."

Hill's robe had been stored in his house in Fort Edward. Although he didn't know for certain who used the robe, it was likely used by his parents in Fort Edward. At one time it had been stored in a railroad livery stable.

The 1956-donated buffalo lap robe is currently on display in "The Age of Horses" exhibit at the Adirondack Museum. The exhibits are currently closed for the season.

Chapter 43

Commemorative Christmas ornament

Commemorating historic buildings with Christmas ornaments is a common practice in many communities throughout the United States. Some organizations sell them annually, and other groups may only issue one celebratory ornament during a milestone or anniversary year.

In the Tri-Lakes region of the Adirondack Park, for example, the Women's Civic Chamber releases an ornament each year depicting a different historic building in the village of Saranac Lake. This year, it's the First United Methodist Church, and the ornament features images of the original church on Main Street and the current one at the corner of Church and St. Bernard streets.

In 1999, the Morehouse Historical Museum in southwestern Hamilton County produced a Christmas tree ornament commemorating the building it calls home—the United Methodist Church, which closed its doors in 1989. While the ornament is certainly not an antique, it is an artifact (No. 2001.17) in the Adirondack Museum's collection (currently in storage).

The Adirondack Museum will sometimes collect items that include souvenir images from the Adirondack region, including Utica Club and Saranac beer memorabilia, according to Chief Curator and Director of Operations Caroline Welsh. Acquiring the Morehouse ornament was important "because of the message that it's sending," she said. Specifically, the artifact commemorates a historic milestone for this building—the creation of the Morehouse Historical Museum.

The ornament, manufactured by Ornaments Unlimited in the United States, was donated to the Adirondack Museum in 2001. It is 4.5 inches tall and 3.25 inches in diameter and is packaged in a red-and-white "Holiday Greetings" box that has windows cut out of each side.

On the white, frosted glass bulb is a scene of the church. "United Methodist Church, Morehouse, NY" is written in green lettering below the drawing, and to the side of the steeple at the top is "1999." A gold-colored metal fixture with a hook is attached to the top.

The church itself is located on state Route 8 in the hamlet of Hoffmeister, in a part of town formerly called Morehouseville. People can see pictures of the church at the Morehouse Historical Museum's Web page, www.rootsweb.com/~nyhamilt/MoreMus/museum.html. Although church services ended in 1989, "In 1999, it was re-opened as

Commemorative Christmas ornament of the United Methodist Church from the Morehouse Historical Museum, artifact No. 2001.17

(Photo courtesy of the Adirondack Museum)

our history museum to hold/display our history records and pictures," the Web page states.

In her publication, "Morehouse Past and Present 1835-1992," Morehouse Town Historian Carol Ford explains the history of churches in the community. There was an Evangelical Lutheran Church and a Roman Catholic Church in the town of Morehouse as early as 1855. In 1866, "the Roman Catholic Church was closed forever under the unhappiest of circumstances," she wrote.

The United Methodist Church began as the Methodist Episcopal Church, which was founded in Morehouseville in the summer of 1881. The Rev. R.O. Beebe, pastor of the Ohio Charge, was the presiding elder of the formation meeting. The exact date of the church's construction, however, is not known. The light fixtures were donated many years ago by Howard and Jenny Remonda Conkling, who owned and operated the Excelsior School of Business in Utica.

"Finally for a lack of attendance, after over a hundred years of service, our church was closed in the summer of 1989," Ford wrote. It was the only church in Morehouse when it closed.

In June 1999, the Morehouse Historical Museum opened its doors to the public in the renovated church, according to a July 27, 1999 article by the Hamilton County News. Planning for a museum began in the mid-1990s, and a few years later, "the old steeple was strengthened and repaired, the building painted, new entry steps constructed and the floor reinforced," the article states. Most of the work was completed by volunteers.

The museum features an oil chandelier (electricity was installed in 1953), the Methodist Episcopal Church organ and altar dressings. Artifacts are placed around the office, and historic photos adorn the walls.

The town of Morehouse was formed in 1835 from the town of Lake Pleasant, and it is named after the first settler, Andrew K. Morehouse, according to the 1872 Gazetteer of the State of New York, by Franklin B. Hough (transcribed on www.rootsweb.com). The town once featured tanneries, sawmills, hotels and more than 300 residents. With a zip code of 13353, Hoffmeister is currently the only post office in the town of Morehouse.

The Morehouse Historical Museum is open from 11 a.m. to 3 p.m. on Saturday and Sunday from Memorial Day weekend to Labor Day weekend.

Chapter 44

Rockwell Kent Christmas Seals poster

The angel of mercy, painted by Rockwell Kent's hand, levitates with her feet pointed toward the Earth and hands extended perpendicular. Dressed in white, as pale as a tuberculosis patient's face, she drops yellow flowers from her palms and suggests that Americans "Buy Christmas Seals, Protect Your Home from Tuberculosis."

The year was 1939, and Kent had been chosen to design the United States Christmas Seals for the National Tuberculosis Association. In November of that year, he presented a copy of his Christmas Seals art to President Franklin D. Roosevelt and Mrs. Ernest Grant, the director of the District of Columbia Tuberculosis Association. A photo of the occasion remains in the Rockwell Kent papers, Archives of American Art, the Smithsonian Institution.

One of Kent's 1939 Christmas Seals posters is artifact No. 2000.40 in the collection of the Adirondack Museum (currently in storage). It was a gift of Scott R. Ferris in memory of Kathleen Kent Finney.

Ferris, an art historian and expert on Kent's career, published the book, "The View from Asgaard: Rockwell Kent's Adirondack Legacy," in 1999 with Alice Gilborn and Adirondack Museum Chief Curator Caroline Welsh. The Museum featured an exhibit with the same title in 1999 and 2000.

Designed in New York City, the poster is 15 inches tall and 11 inches wide. The angel is placed in the top right-hand corner, in front of a red double-barred cross and a blue background. The text, in white letters, is in the bottom left-hand corner.

The 1939 poster's design was similar to the actual Christmas Seals stamps, sold to "stamp out tuberculosis." The Seals—17.5-by-23 mm or 3/4-by-15/16 inches—featured the head and upper torso of the angel in the bottom right-hand corner, the year "1939" in the top right-hand corner, the red double-barred cross in the top left-hand corner, and a blue background.

The 1939 Christmas Seals were manufactured in sheets of 100 (10-by-10), and 96 of the Seals were of Kent's design. The four in the center were called Slogan Seals and were designed by Earl Hoffman. No. 45 on the sheet had a light blue background and stated "Health to All." No. 46, "Protect Your Home from Tuberculosis," had a pink background. No. 55 was also pink and stated, "Tuberculosis

National Tuberculosis Association Christmas Seals poster from 1939,
artifact No. 2000.40, illustrated by Rockwell Kent
*(Courtesy of the Plattsburgh State Art Museum, Plattsburgh College Foundation,
Rockwell Kent Gallery and Collection, Bequest of Sally Kent Gordon)*

Preventable Curable." And No. 56, a light blue Seal, simply wished everyone "Holiday Greetings."

Tuberculosis, or TB, was once the leading cause of death in the United States. It is a disease caused by bacteria called mycobacterium tuberculosis (tubercle bacillus), which usually attacks the lungs but can infect any part of the body, according to the Centers for Disease Control and Prevention. It is an airborne disease spread by coughing or sneezing.

In 1882, German physician and scientist Robert Koch discovered tubercle bacillus and published his findings. An Adirondack transplant from New York City, Dr. Edward Livingston Trudeau, was inspired by Koch's research.

Trudeau, who had suffered from tuberculosis since 1871, had moved to the Adirondack Mountains to spend the last years of his life, but he found that the clean, mountain air made him feel better. He had heard of a successful TB sanitarium in Europe, and with Koch's papers in hand, a "cured" Trudeau began his own research in a laboratory and founded the Adirondack Cottage Sanitarium in 1884 in Saranac Lake—the first of its kind in the United States. His one-room "Little Red" cottage is now located at the Trudeau Institute, and the sprawling Trudeau Sanatorium, on the side of Mount Pisgah, is currently occupied by the American Management Association.

Soon after Trudeau's success, sanitariums were being built across the United States to battle the TB epidemic, and a national organization was founded. In 1904, the National Association for the Study and Prevention of Tuberculosis was created. The name was changed to the National Tuberculosis Association in 1918 and changed again to the National Tuberculosis and Respiratory Disease Association in 1968. In 1973, the name was changed to its final incarnation, the American Lung Association, which continues to sell Christmas Seals, even online (www.lungusa.org) with e-cards to "help kids cope with their asthma and help adults facing lung cancer and emphysema."

The first Christmas Seals in the United States were designed in 1907 by Emily Bissell, who was inspired by a similar fund-raising program in Denmark. Bissell was active in the American Red Cross, and her cousin was a doctor at a TB hospital in Delaware. The first stamp, with a red cross centered in a half-wreath of holly above the words "Merry Christmas" was sold on Dec. 7, 1907 in Wilmington, Del. By the end of the holiday season, Bissell had sold her first 50,000 and printed 50,000 more, according to the American Lung Association. Even President Theodore Roosevelt endorsed the campaign.

In 1907, about 17.4 million Americans died from tuberculosis, according to the U.S. Bureau of the Census (transcribed on www.healthsentinel.com). In 1939, when Rockwell Kent designed the Christmas Seals, TB killed 4.7 million Americans. By the late 1940s, new TB-fighting drugs were introduced, and the cases declined sharply in the U.S. Many sanatoriums (as they were spelled by that time) closed in communities such as Saranac Lake, and the focus of the National Tuberculosis Association shifted to other respiratory diseases, hence the name change to the American Lung Association.

Kent only designed one set of Christmas Seals in his lifetime. Born in Tarrytown Heights, N.Y. in 1882, he was an accomplished painter and illustrator by the time he bought Asgaard Farm near Au Sable Forks in 1927. Kent won commissions to paint wall murals at public buildings, galleries and museums. He made illustrations for billboards, printed pages and the popular press, including the covers of *Scribner's* magazine and the 1939 "Home Decorator and Color Guide" for Sherwin-Williams. Kent was well-known as an artist, an author and a political activist. He died in Plattsburgh in 1971.

After his death, the rights to Kent's artwork and writings were conveyed to his widow, Shirley (Sally) Kent. Upon her death in 2000, ownership of the rights to the artwork and writings of Rockwell Kent were conveyed to the Plattsburgh College Foundation to benefit the Plattsburgh State Art Museum, Rockwell Kent Gallery and Collection.

This 1939 poster is reproduced by permission of the Plattsburgh State Art Museum, Rockwell Kent Gallery and Collection.

Chapter 45

Land of Makebelieve souvenirs

As the year 2003 fades away, it's an appropriate time to reflect on the loss of an Adirondack legend, Upper Jay artist and toymaker Arto Monaco, who died on Nov. 20, 2003 at the age of 90. He is best known for creating a 12-acre theme park, the Land of Makebelieve, on the East Branch of the Ausable River in Essex County.

Born on Nov. 15, 1913 in Au Sable Forks, Monaco lived in Elizabethtown and then Upper Jay, where his father owned a general store and a restaurant.

Monaco's life changed when he met artist Rockwell Kent, who lived at nearby Asgaard Farm and ate regularly at Monaco's restaurant. After working with Kent, graduating from the Pratt Institute in New York City, working in Hollywood, and serving in the U.S. Army during World War II, Monaco returned home to his beloved Adirondack Mountains in the late 1940s (Adirondack Life, June 2001).

Monaco established Arto Monaco's Toy Company and helped Julian Reiss by designing Santa's Workshop (open in 1949) in the town of Wilmington and Old McDonald's Farm in Lake Placid. In 1954, it was Monaco's turn to open his own theme park, the Land of Makebelieve, on Route 9N in Upper Jay.

The Land of Makebelieve closed in 1979 after its buildings had been ruined by repeated flooding (11 times in 25 years) along the Ausable River, but not after thousands of children and adults were treated to the musings of this highly creative man. The Land of Makebelieve was Monaco's kingdom, and he was the humble leader.

In 2001, Monaco donated several Land of Makebelieve items to the Adirondack Museum collection. Among the artifacts are two 1975 coloring books (No. 2001.57.1 and No. 2001.57.2) and a 1975 coloring desk tray (No. 2001.57.3).

The coloring books have red, white, yellow and black covers. The plastic desk tray is white and has the words "Land of Makebelieve, Upper Jay, New York" printed in black on the front. There is also a printed scene of the Land of Makebelieve that is colorable. Red, blue, yellow, green and brown colored pencils are included with yellow paper instructions and a black plastic easel so the tray can be displayed on a wall or a counter. The entire coloring tray package is covered in shrink-wrap.

The Adirondack Museum's librarian keeps files on the most well-

A 1975 coloring desk tray, artifact No. 2001.57.3, from the Land of Makebelieve, operated by Arto Monaco from 1954 to 1979, in the Essex County hamlet of Upper Jay. Monaco died on Nov. 20, 2003 at the age of 90.

(Photo courtesy of the Adirondack Museum)

known Adirondack personalities, including Monaco. Articles about the artist from Adirondack Life and the Lake Placid News are in the library's folder, as is a miniature photo album published by Life magazine.

The Life album begins: "Upper Jay, N.Y.—Pert and pint-size, the Land of Make Believe invites moppets into a wild West saloon to belly up to a two-foot-high bar for (soft) drinks, or ride a tiny stern-wheeler, the Billabong Belle. Characters in Aesop's fables and Mother Goose rhymes are all built in Lilliputian models."

In the album are pictures of Cactus Flats—a miniature western town—and the fairytale castle. It shows kids enjoying the safari and a ride on the Billabong Belle, a 22-foot-long riverboat that transported up to 30 young passengers on the Makebelieve pond.

"Most of the delights of this improbable world are the work of the hand and mind of Arto Monaco, who is president (not king, as you might expect), of the Land of Makebelieve," the Life album continued. "Mr. Monaco's artistic powers have produced toys and books and movie sets. His reputation as a creator of fanciful villages is widespread, for he has designed four others: a Santa's workshop, a ghost town, an adventure town, and a gaslight village."

The Museum's file on Monaco also includes a copy of the four-page Cactus Flats Gazette, published "every now and then." In this paper—the Ox Cart Edition—printed in the "summer of 1881" when the weather was "Wet'n Dry," anyone could have picked up the paper "fer free."

The headline for one of the top stories, edited by Leo Kaplan, was, "Card Game Ends in Shootin' Spree." The newspaper was filled with advertisements, one for Robinson Rifles and another for the Artistic Tonsorial Saloon, with the "only bathtub this side of Dodge City." Performances at the Cactus Flats Theater featured Saddlebag Sadie, "Star Troupe" and The 4 Johns (Zachay John, Straight John, Mackinnon John and Manning John).

In the coloring books, Monaco drew characters and objects from the Land of Makebelieve: Sir Bulbnose, Freddie the Friendly Dragon, Peter Peters, Mary Mary, the queen's coach, the overland stage and the Billabong Belle. There were connect-the-dot drawings, crossword puzzles and games such as tic-tac-toe to keep the children busy on the ride home.

The property itself was magical. There was a railroad station, a barber shop, a general store, a firehouse, and homes for Peter Pumpkin Eater, the Three Bears and the Queen of Hearts.

"Each building has for tiny tots, so very, very much," the Life album stated. "And yet there's not a single sign that says, 'Hey, kids—don't touch.'"

In addition to his family, Monaco is survived by thousands of children who walked through the gates of the Land of Makebelieve over its 25-year life. Some of these grown-up children may even have Monaco-made coloring books and other souvenirs in their closets. The ones at the Adirondack Museum are kept in a drawer for safe keeping.

To learn more about Monaco, read the Adirondack Life online feature, "Upper Jay Mourns Arto Monaco," at www.adirondacklife.com. The Web site also includes a link to Anne Mackinnon's June 2001 story titled, "From Tinseltown to the Land of Makebelieve: A portrait of Upper Jay's old master."

Source attributions for the "Adirondack Attic" columns can be found in each chapter. Much of the information was derived from the artifacts' accession files at the Adirondack Museum.

photo by Andy Flynn

As a boy, Theodore Roosevelt watched birds in these woods near Black Pond while staying at the Paul Smith's Hotel in the 1870s, before the land became Paul Smith's College property.

Index

A

A&E, 1
Aber, Ted, 106
Acetylene generator, 107-109
Adams, Thomas, 26
Adams New York No. 1 gum, 26
Adirondac, hamlet of, 16
Adirondack & St. Lawrence Line, 46
Adirondack Arms Company, 97-98
Adirondack Arrow, 18
Adirondack Carousel, 27
Adirondack Centennial Railroad, 48
Adirondack chair, 59-61
Adirondack Community College, 74
Adirondack Cottage (Adirondack
    Museum), 61
Adirondack Cottage Sanitarium, 128
Adirondack Daily Enterprise, 2
Adirondack Division (New York
    Central), 46-48
Adirondack 46'ers, 75
Adirondack guide, 49-51, 86-88
Adirondack Historical Association,
    122
Adirondack Iron & Steel Company,
    17
Adirondack Iron Works, 51
Adirondack Life, 25, 62, 98-99,
    130-132
Adirondack Mountain Club, 67, 75
Adirondack Mountain Reserve, 3
Adirondack Mountain Spinners, 111
"Adirondack Mountains, New York,"
    painting, 34-35
Adirondack Museum Historic Photo
    Collection, 49
Adirondack Museum library, 55, 56,
    58, 130
Adirondack Museum on Main Store
    and Gallery, 43

"Adirondack Outfittings" catalog,
    59-60
"Adirondack Prints and Printmakers:
    The Call of the Wild," 68-69
Adirondack Railroad, 46-48
Adirondack Railway Corporation, 48
Adirondack Railway Preservation
    Society, 48
Adirondack Regional Tourism
    Council, 1
Adirondack Scenic Railroad, 48
Adirondack Trail Improvement
    Society, 65
"Adirondack Yesteryears," 1
"Adirondacks: Illustrated," The, 86
"Adirondacks in the Age of Horses"
    exhibit, 80
Adirondak Loj, 51
"Adventures in the Wilderness," 22,
    34
"Age of Horses," The, 122
Aide memoire, 15-16
Aiden Lair hotel, 82
Albany, city of, 15, 57
Alessi, Doreen, 120
Alger, Mrs. William Cummings, 8
Algonquin Peak, 16
Alice T. Miner Museum, 111
"Alta Cliff" Cottage, 56
Altamont Milk Company, 19
American Alpine Club, 65
American Arts and Crafts Movement,
    112-114
American Buffalo Robe Co., 122
American Canoe Association, 45
American Chemical Society, 107
American Lung Association, 128-129
American Management Association,
    128
American Museum of Natural
    History, 30

Outhouse along the Northville-Placid Trail near Long Lake

Old stove in woods near a former Tupper Lake logging operation

photo by Andy Flynn

Stream at the former hydroelectric site for the Saranac Inn resort

The Adirondack Museum

The Adirondack Museum is a regional history and art museum, located in New York state's Hamilton County, which interprets the Adirondack Park and greater North Country region. Originally the idea of mining executive, philanthropist, preservationist and local historian Harold K. Hochschild (1892-1981), the Museum is located on the site of the former Blue Mountain House resort hotel (1876-1950). The Museum was chartered by the New York State Education Department in 1948 and opened to the public in 1957.

The Adirondack Museum's mission is to explore and present the human, cultural and environmental history of the Adirondacks, and it has consistently employed state-of-the-art exhibits, programs and interpretive and curatorial practices. The 205-acre campus features 42 buildings and includes 25 indoor and outdoor exhibition, education and study/storage spaces.

The Adirondack Museum is noted for its 19th and 20th century art collection by famous painters such as Thomas Cole, Winslow Homer, Arthur Fitzwilliam Tait, Frederic Remington, Harold Weston and Rockwell Kent. Object collections include tools for trades and industries, land and water vehicles, works of fine and folk art, and artifacts representing domestic life, community, sport and recreation. Other holdings include books, documents, historic photographs, films and ephemera, as well as significant audio and oral history collections. Its large boat collection contains many examples of the region's signature artifact—the Adirondack guideboat. The rustic furniture and decorative arts collection features objects unique to the region.

More than 115,000 people visit the Adirondack Museum annually, including about 90,000 visitors during the five-month season when the campus is open to the public (mid-May to mid-October). The remainder of the year, the facility caters to researchers, school groups and Adirondack residents attending special events such as the Cabin Fever lectures at the end of each winter.

For more information about the Adirondack Museum, call (518) 352-7311 or log on to the Web site at www.adirondackmuseum.org. The Museum is located on state Route 30 in the hamlet of Blue Mountain Lake. ˙

154

The Author

Andy Flynn is a freelance writer, photographer and editor living in Saranac Lake. His syndicated column, "Adirondack Attic," runs in five newspapers in northern New York. In 2004, he founded Hungry Bear Publishing.

During the day, Flynn is employed as the Senior Public Information Specialist for the New York State Adirondack Park Agency Visitor Interpretive Centers (VICs) at Paul Smiths and Newcomb. He is a Certified Interpretive Guide with the National Association for Interpretation.

Flynn is an award-winning journalist, garnering merits of excellence from the National Newspaper Association, New York Newspaper Publishers Association and the New York Press Association (NYPA) for photography, headline writing, editorial writing, news writing, feature writing, front-page layout and community service reporting. He was the 1996 NYPA Writer of the Year for weekly New York state newspapers with circulations under 10,000.

Flynn's freelance activities include editing and layout for the Adirondack Daily Enterprise's Winter Guide and Summer Guide and editing and layout for regional book projects, such as Charles Brumley's 2003 collection of short stories, "Cry Me Home, Loon: Adirondack Stories."

Before joining the VIC staff, he was a writer and editor for the Adirondack Daily Enterprise in Saranac Lake and the Lake Placid News, a correspondent for the Plattsburgh Press-Republican, an announcer for WNBZ 1240-AM in Saranac Lake, and a general assignment news reporter and radio documentary producer for North Country Public Radio in Canton. He is a graduate of the SUNY College at Fredonia and the Tupper Lake High School.

The Final Chapter

Before I began writing the "Adirondack Attic" columns in 2003,
I dabbled in various disciplines of prose, including fiction.
Adding my short story, "The Glove," to this compilation was
an afterthought, but I believe it accurately represents my
approach to writing about artifacts in the Adirondack Museum.
The object, a glove, leads us to an understanding of the former owner.
At the same time, during that physical and emotional journey, we
find out more about ourselves, our neighbors and our community.
We learn that there is more to objects, and people, than meets the eye.

The Glove

Robbie didn't go to the funeral, and he hadn't been to the old neighborhood since his freshman year in college, when he moved his mother across town seven years earlier. He plunked the phone down on the coffee table and scratched his head.

A lawyer had just invited him back to the street where he grew up, to the yellow and brown house next to his childhood home. Something about a will and divvying up assets. He barely knew the woman.

Mrs. Peterson lived in a neat two-story home with a spacious front porch, a painting studio attached to the back of the house and a dilapidated garage in the far end of the yard where her gardens grew. On both sides of the yard were cedar hedges that kept away peering eyes and wandering children. A space between one hedge and a white pine tree on the left side of the yard led to the driveway next door, to Robbie's former house. That's how he used to visit the old lady. He and his brothers were the only ones allowed to walk through the yard and knock on the back door when they visited.

Robbie didn't remember much of Mrs. Peterson. She had white hair, a lot of wrinkles and red cheeks. She always wore a sweater, and her house smelled like a church with cats in every pew. She painted landscapes of the surrounding mountains, lakes and rivers and sold her work in the library's art show every summer. He only remembered one work, an oil painting of Buttermilk Falls near Long Lake. Mrs. Peterson was generous with her chocolate chip cookies but stingy with her money.

"Only 25 cents for raking the entire yard?!" Robbie once complained to his mother. "Other kids get way more money than that. I should at least get two dollars for the whole day. That's a cheap old lady."

Robbie was too shy and too afraid to ask Mrs. Peterson for a raise. One time she yelled at a couple of neighborhood kids who crossed her lawn. Of course they were wrong by stealing rhubarb from the garden, but to a child, her yelling created the "old lady" reputation. She was as old as Grandma but not as sweet; Grandma never yelled.

That didn't stop Robbie from running to Mrs. Peterson's house every time he fought with his brothers. She was the only friend he had. Robbie was the youngest of three boys, and the fighting was always his fault. At least that's what his father kept telling him.

"I want to move in with you," an 8-year-old Robbie told Mrs. Peterson after one bad fight.

Tears ran down his face as he sat in a red vinyl chair at the kitchen table, a calico cat rubbing against his legs, purring and pawing at his pants for attention. With a plate full of cookies in front of his face, Robbie fed himself with one hand and drank milk from a glass with the other. It wasn't the bland, industrial-tasting instant milk his parents made him drink; it was rich and creamy whole milk, and Mrs. Peterson let him mix liquid Hershey's chocolate in the glass. He relished gulping down the milk and scooping out the glob of chocolate at the bottom. It was a child's elixir, and the pain subsided, at least for a few minutes. Mrs. Peterson sat down next to Robbie. Sipping orange pekoe tea and petting a Siamese cat on her lap, she soaked in the moment.

— — —

To Robbie, his visits to the old lady next door were distant memories. Baseball card gum soon satisfied his sweet tooth instead of chocolate chip cookies, and school, household chores and baseball games occupied most of his time. Before he knew it, he was grown up—high school, college, a job writing for the regional newspaper.

Work was Robbie's life, and he rarely had time for friends or family, never mind memories. He was always thinking ahead, trying to get the scoop, working hard to become the best journalist in the Adirondacks.

Robbie was cursed with endless energy. At age 22, he suffered a "young-life crisis" after finishing four-and-a-half years of college and returning home to the mountains. It was a damp December day, and he walked his old newspaper route along the shore of Raquette Pond. This was where he wrote in private, jotting down poetry, lyrics and essays while examining the clouds as they raced the blowing snow across the frozen pond. In the distance a single-lane snowmobile highway penetrated the community of ice shanties where people escaped their everyday lives to catch a northern pike or two.

This was Robbie's retreat, and the landscape had changed little after five years. The trees were simply larger, and the rocks were that much smaller.

Robbie spent his teenage years planning his escape, dreaming of the time he could get the farthest away from his family and the town that smothered his creativity and ambitions. After high school graduation, he was the first kid to run out of the school's door and greet the world.

College life changed Robbie. He had grown fond of the woods and waters during his senior year, traveling home as often as he could to escape the hubbub of society. This time he came home for good. He had always enjoyed the outdoor life. In fact, he used to walk through the snow and the wind and below-zero temperatures delivering newspapers until he couldn't feel his legs anymore. The freedom to think and create in this frozen tundra devoid of criticism and failure was the highlight of his youth. It was his religion. The painful part of returning from a snowy paper route was going inside the house, where a thousand needles pricked his red-glowing legs until they reached room temperature. Then, when it seemed as though everything was better, he spent an hour scratching both legs until they were numb again.

Beyond the slush-covered rocks lining the pond road, Robbie kicked crusty snow off a private dock on the shoreline, watching darkness overcome the whitewashed winter scene. Lights from the boulevard glowed in the distance, painting the sky shades of orange and gray.

When he returned from college, Robbie realized that his life was just beginning. Uncertainty was on the horizon, and fear and panic boiled inside his churning stomach.

Time spent at this welcome-home retreat—the warmth of familiar territory and the birthplace of his ambitions—distilled those useless gases of worry into droplets of concentrated energy. He knew that this nitro would be needed to go back into the cold weather and make something of himself. Life in the real world began at dawn.

— — —

By the end of her life, Mrs. Peterson only had memories to keep her company. She rarely saw her grandchildren. Her only daughter, Julie, moved to California after graduating from college, and she returned home every two or three years. Her sister, Elizabeth, called every Sunday but rarely traveled from her New Hampshire home. Mrs. Peterson's husband, Frank, was long gone, having died in Italy during World War II. An expert skier, he joined the U.S. Army's 10th Mountain Division in 1942 and fought Nazis in the Italian snowcapped mountains in 1944. He only used his skis once during battle; it was the last day of his life.

Mrs. Peterson was in her landscape studio when she received the telegram. A stream of tears flowed down her face and dripped onto the golden head of her four-year-old daughter, whom she squeezed until her fingers were as white as gesso. After a week of grieving and settling her husband's affairs, Mrs. Peterson cleaned up his wood shop in the garage. She gave away everything, from the tiniest screwdriver to Frank's furniture-making table saw.

Days later, she painted her husband's portrait. He was standing under the canopy of the Junction train station, handsomely dressed in a green Army uniform, with their 8-year-old daughter on his shoulders. She painted a smile on his face. That's how she wanted to remember him.

Before she knew it, Mrs. Peterson had painted another portrait of her husband, this time fishing, and another as a high school football star. When Julie began questioning the man in the paintings, a man she didn't remember, Mrs. Peterson moved the portraits to the garage, locked the door and hid the key.

Mrs. Peterson spent 40 years teaching English in the local high school. After she retired, she volunteered for the elementary school reading program, coached young actors in the high school drama club and joined the Adult Center as the coordinator of birthday parties. She was busier at age 65 than she was at 45.

Still, true friendship eluded her. She was more interested in helping her community than wasting quality time over a cup of coffee and a game of hearts. Decades before her retirement, she accepted a patriotic widow's sentence of life without parole, stuck in a yellow-and-brown house symbolically waiting for her true love to return from war.

When she wasn't volunteering somewhere, she was either meandering through mountain passes with her camera or painting oil landscapes in her studio.

Although she didn't have pictures of all the people who had been important in her life, she could recall people's faces with a photographic memory. Her days were filled with re-living her wedding day, Christmas mornings with her daughter and trips to Ottawa with her sister.

When the sun went down, especially in the gloomy winter months, Mrs. Peterson escaped to her other world, staying up until 3 a.m. and making morning coffee before dawn. Driving down the road of life, she had passed countless pillars of sleepless nights and could barely recognize the blur of days dangling in between. Like a vampire, her body came to life at sundown, and in the cloak of darkness she retreated to the garage for a love affair she kept secret until the day she died.

At 75 years old, Mrs. Peterson lived longer than she had expected. When she was 70, the doctor found a tumor on her left breast, but after a mastectomy and chemotherapy, she went into remission. By mud season, she was getting sick again and started making plans to give away her small fortune. Arrangements were completed by June, but she passed away before saying good-bye to her loved ones.

— — —

Robbie parked his blue 1990 Pontiac Sunbird in front of Mrs. Peterson's house, taking a deep breath before getting out of the car and ringing the doorbell. It was the first time he had used the front entrance, and he fumbled his car keys while juggling a vase of lilies and a Hallmark sympathy card. Mrs. Peterson's daughter answered the door and invited him inside the living room where the lawyer was about to read Mrs. Peterson's last will and testament. Julie's two grownup children were sitting next to Aunt Elizabeth. Julie flew in from California without a husband; they had divorced a few years earlier. The kids, Tom and Sarah, were in their mid-twenties and lived close to their mother's home in Tahoe City.

"Hi, I'm Robbie," he said, handing Julie the vase and card. "Sorry for not coming to the funeral yesterday. I had to cover a village board meeting."

"That's okay. I understand." Julie said, pointing to the living room. "Right in here. Make yourself at home."

John Ritenouer, a lanky 80-year-old attorney who reeked of cigarette smoke, read the will with a raspy voice.

"Julie gets the house and $10,000. Elizabeth gets the landscape paintings, $20,000 and the cats. The kids get $5,000 apiece."

"Cats?" Aunt Elizabeth said. "I don't want those damn cats."

"Hush, let the man finish," Julie said. "We'll take care of it later."

The lawyer handed Robbie a shoebox covered with New York Mets wrapping paper.

"Here you go, son. This is for you."

"Okay," Robbie said slowly, squinting his eyes with curiosity. "This is a little strange. What's in the box?"

"I don't know, son. Open it and find out."

All eyes in the room watched Robbie's hands untie the white ribbon and tear the orange-and-blue wrapping paper off the box. He lifted the top and looked inside.

"Hm," Robbie said, listing all the contents in the box as he took them out and placed them on the glass coffee table.

"A leather glove, for the right hand. An envelope with a card inside. And an old letter."

"What does the letter say?" asked Aunt Elizabeth, who was never shy about asking Mrs. Peterson for a weekly update on local gossip. "Just curious."

Just nosy is more like it, Robbie thought.

"Son, you don't have to read it now," the lawyer said.

"No, I don't mind," he said, glancing at Aunt Elizabeth. Robbie unfolded the crumpled paper. "It's from a kid ... hmm ... It's from me."

"What's it say?" Aunt Elizabeth asked.

"Shush," said Julie.

"Dear Mom," Robbie began. "I ran away from home. I want to live with Mrs. Peterson. She is the best. My brothers are mean and nobody likes me. Robbie."

"You never lived here," Aunt Elizabeth snapped.

"Yeh, I know. It must have been after a fight at home or something. That's weird. She kept it all those years."

"What's the note say?" asked Aunt Elizabeth.

Robbie opened the light blue envelope. The card had a homemade oil painting of a boy with a wooden baseball bat on his shoulder and a baseball glove hanging from the end. On the bottom right corner were the blue-painted words, "Alice Peterson."

"Dear Robbie. I never forgot the friendship we shared long ago, and I think of you often. You are so busy with your work that I fear a phone call from me would just bother you. I have fond memories of your visits, chocolate milk and cookies and the time you wanted to live with me. Those were happy days."

Robbie turned the card over.

"I have some more gifts for you. I want you to have all the contents of my portrait studio in the garage. You'll find everything you need to live a happy and healthy life. Love, Mrs. Peterson."

Robbie put the card down and picked up the well-worn, brown glove, splattered with a swatch-load of oil paint.

"That's Alice's other painting glove," said Aunt Elizabeth, pointing at Robbie's hand. "We looked for it for days and thought it was lost. We buried her with the left-hand glove. It was her wish."

"She has a portrait studio?" Robbie asked Aunt Elizabeth. "I thought she only painted landscapes."

"So did I," Aunt Elizabeth said.

"Me too," said Julie.

They all looked at each other, paused, then scrambled for the back door. Julie led the way. As she approached her mother's landscape studio, she peered at the gloomy garage through the window. The smell of paint and linseed oil permeated the air. Then, one by one, they filed onto the asphalt driveway.

Robbie carried Mrs. Peterson's glove in his left hand. As he passed the screen door, it twitched. When he stepped onto the driveway, he looked at the glove and dismissed the strange movement. His hand must have brushed the door on his way out.

In single file, with Julie leading the way and Robbie in the rear, they walked through the back yard to the garage.

Black shingles were peeling off the edges of the sunken roof, which had been plastered with thick tar to prevent leaks. Brown paint flakes curled along the trim.

The glove twitched again, and the soft, leather fingers slowly began filling up like a balloon. The glove expanded slightly every step Robbie made. He didn't even notice.

Robbie's eyes were fixed on the garage, and he began to think of this building as a character in one of his newspaper articles. Neglected. An eyesore. Something that should be torn down. Old face. Sad eyes. Someone who should be thrown into a nursing home. All the glass in the building was painted black to keep out the sunlight. It was dark and gloomy, and if it were gone today, nobody would miss it.

The glove began to squeeze harder as if someone was holding Robbie's hand. He still didn't notice. His mind was on the historic structure in front of him.

In a way, Robbie felt sorry for the building. It made him think of his grandmother, who died several years earlier. She grew old with only cigarettes and Lawrence Welk to keep her company. Visits became rare as he and his brothers grew up and began leaving home. When she died of lung cancer, he wept for days. It was the first time he had to deal with a death in the family.

The glove comforted Robbie as his eyes scanned the garage. Wild hops covered the entire left side and crept onto the roof. Planters that once held beautiful marigolds and impatiens were now empty and rotting. The mulch pile next to the garage reeked of fermented cantaloupe rinds, celery, leaves and dead rodents. (Mrs. Peterson threw her cats' prizes in the pile.)

By the time they reached the garage and began staring at the padlock on the side door, Mrs. Peterson's painting glove was firmly planted on Robbie's hand. When he stopped, he felt the pressure, and a chill shot through his brain and down his torso. For a split second, it seemed as though his face detached from his body, turned around, and levitated in front of his head. Something strange had just happened. An out-of-body experience? Dizzy, he shook his head and jerked his eyes down to the glove.

It was deflated. Just a glove. The pressure was gone, but his hand still throbbed.

"Okay," Julie said, frustrated and yanking on the padlock. "Who has the key to this thing?"

"I don't," said the lawyer.

"Not me," Aunt Elizabeth said and pointed to Robbie. "How about Mr. Lucky Pants over here."

"I don't have it."

Suddenly a key fell from the glove and landed on Robbie's foot. Picking it up, he said, "Well, I guess I do have it. See if this works." Robbie handed the key to the lawyer, who opened the door, walked in and turned on the light.

— — —

The group filed into the cluttered garage and gawked at hundreds of oil-painted portraits that filled every corner. Some were piled vertically and some were leaning against the pink support beams and the walls, which were painted as mountain and river landscapes from around the region. Other portraits were stacked horizontally on yellow card tables. A red ladder led to the baby blue loft, where even more portraits were stored. Birds and clouds were painted on the ceiling, and native fish were painted on the cement floor as if the slab was a see-through Adirondack aquarium with rainbow trout and yellow perch.

"Jesus," Julie said, sifting through the framed portraits, instinctively looking for herself.

These were people Mrs. Peterson had known and loved all of her life. She painted from memory, trying to capture each friend and family member in the setting that most fit their personality.

Julie walked to the pile next to her mother's easel and said, "Oh my God. Tom, Sarah, come here."

Julie lifted a fresh painting of her and the kids holding luggage on a tarmac, with jets in the background. The title, "Homecoming," was painted on the back.

All eyes were on this pile as Mrs. Peterson's final memories were revealed.

"Hello, Lizzy!" Aunt Elizabeth exclaimed.

Next in line was a recent portrait of Aunt Elizabeth, with binoculars around her neck and a moose eating from a swamp. Her favorite pastime was "Moose Hunting" with her friends on the back roads of Berlin. She picked up the painting and admired the detail.

"I'm wearing my favorite sweater," Aunt Elizabeth said. "How did she know?"

The next painting was of the lawyer wearing a black suit and a red necktie, reading Mrs. Peterson's last will and testament under ominous thunderclouds. Standing next to him was the funeral director, who was also wearing a black suit and a red necktie. He was holding a bill and smiling. The lawyer's bill was in his coat pocket. "Business is Good" was the title.

"This doesn't look like me," Mr. Ritenouer said, straightening his blue necktie. "And the bill's in the mail, not in my coat pocket!"

Since the backyard studio and all its contents were now Robbie's property, Mrs. Peterson had propped up his portrait on the paint-stained workbench, leaning it against the black glass. In the painting, Robbie wore a shirt and tie and held a pen and reporter's notepad while interviewing the governor. "Getting There" was the title.

On the workbench in front of the framed portrait was a forest green scrapbook with a white label that read "ROBBIE MARTIN."

All eyes were on Robbie's book, and the group huddled around him.

"What's in it?" asked Aunt Elizabeth.

He opened the book and found newspaper articles from his life, starting when he was a kid next door. There was news of the Little League all-star baseball team, 4-H club, honor rolls, musical productions, varsity baseball team, high school and college graduations and his journalism career. There were two years' worth of clippings from the newspaper where he worked. All the articles had red markings on them with constructive criticism.

The last page was a note critiquing Robbie's work. It was written shortly before Mrs. Peterson's death; the last clipping was published the day she left for the hospital for the final operation. Robbie read the letter aloud.

"On the whole, your writing is good, but it has no soul. Where are the people? Their feelings? Their toils and triumphs? Life isn't about garbage and sewer rates and traffic accidents. It is about the people who live through the garbage, the sewer rates and the traffic accidents. (over)"

Robbie lifted his head and looked at the painting. A closer inspection revealed that the governor's family was in the background waiting for him next to a limousine. Robbie turned the note over and finished reading it.

"Use your words to paint portraits of the people you get to know. When you're my age, those memories will be all you have left. Love, Mrs. Peterson."

— — —

Over the next hour, Robbie and Mrs. Peterson's family discovered more portraits of themselves, mostly from their youth. In Robbie's other painting, he was a 10-year-old boy wearing an orange baseball uniform, an aluminum bat in one hand and a first baseman's glove in the other. There were baby images of Tom and Sarah. Julie was a high school graduate, a basketball player and a ballerina. Aunt Elizabeth was a young nurse in a U.S. Navy uniform, a teenager climbing a high peak and a 12-year-old girl riding a horse. Dozens of Frank Peterson's portraits were found: underneath the workbench, up in the loft, and inside the 1940 four-door Buick Woodie she permanently parked in the garage the day the government telegram arrived.

Locking the door behind Aunt Elizabeth, Robbie said, "There's a portrait of everyone except Mrs. Peterson in there."

"She was a good woman," Aunt Elizabeth said with tears in her eyes, squeezing Robbie's hand as they walked back to the house. "A little nuts, but a good woman."

— — —

The next day, Robbie's newspaper ran a feature story about Mrs. Peterson on the obituary page, complete with two photos—one of her in the landscape studio and one of the interior of the backyard portrait studio packed with dust-covered paintings.

"Tupper Woman Leaves Legacy of Love" was the headline, by ROBERT J. MARTIN, Staff Writer.

Groggy from staying up all night, Robbie took a clipping of the article and taped it to Mrs. Peterson's headstone in the St. Alphonsus Cemetery. He stood on fresh sod. Wind rustled through the leaves, and a robin hopped along the sun-bathed ground looking for worms.

"Mrs. Peterson," he wrote in red ink on the clipping. "Thanks for the cookies. Your friend, Robbie."

After a soft "See you later" passed through his lips, he climbed into his new Buick and adjusted the rear-view mirror, where press credentials and a paint-stained leather glove dangled in the wind. A yellow Post-It note on his black digital camera case read, "Buy cat food." Robbie rolled down the driver's-side window and headed back to the office.

photo by Andy Flynn

Pine trees near Tupper Lake